# *Wicked* WILMINGTON DELAWARE

KEVIN MCGONEGAL

THE
History
PRESS

Published by The History Press
Charleston, SC
www.historypress.com

First published 2021

ISBN 9781540248763

Library of Congress Control Number: 2021937191

# CONTENTS

# ACKNOWLEDGEMENTS

This book is a collection of stories I've written over thirty years, sometimes for various publications but most of all for my own enjoyment. My siblings and I were raised on stories told by our father about his life growing up in Wilmington, Delaware. Once described in an article in the *Philadelphia Daily News* as a "storyteller of the old Gaelic fire-hearth mold," Dad remains my inspiration to try to tell an interesting tale.

I am forever grateful to the wonderful staffs at the Delaware Historical Society (DHS), Hagley Museum and Library and Delaware Public Archives (DPA) for their assistance on practically all of the stories included here. In particular, I want to thank former DHS curator Connie Cooper and current curator Leigh Rifenburg, Hagley staffer Angela Schad, and Bruce Haase and Connor Graham from DPA.

"Bookies, Bawdy Houses and Chief Black" started with some comments by my father about his father's chosen profession and his interaction with the police. I was able to work some of Dad's anecdotes into the narrative. Special thanks go to Lisa Hemphill and Joseph Sammons of the Wilmington Police Department for their assistance. Former Wilmington police officer Tom Monahan helped put Chief Black into proper perspective, and my former boss the late Mayor Bill McLaughlin supplied me with great stories of growing up on Wilmington's east side. Also, Carol Hoffecker's book *Corporate Capital* was an invaluable resource.

The Three Gun Wilson story was grounded in the research materials available at Hagley Museum and Library, particularly the copy of Harold

"Three Gun" Wilson's book about his exploits in Wilmington. John Medkeff Jr., author of *Brewing in Delaware*, provided me with needed background on the state of the industry before and after Prohibition and assisted with finding images to accompany the story. Daniel Okrent's book, *Last Call: The Rise and Fall of Prohibition*, helped put Delaware's Prohibition experience in a broader perspective and gave insight into Pierre S. du Pont's motivations.

"The Cop and the Incorrigible" also grew out of my father's stories, these about his boyhood friend Tom Conaty. The Conaty sons, Tom, Bill and Gerry, and in particular their mother, the late Louise Conaty Wachter Hoffman, were essential to this effort, and I am grateful for their numerous contributions. Tom Conaty's former partner, the late George McLaughlin, gave me great insight into police work in the 1940s and how fellow officers reacted to the Conaty murder. Former city treasurer Henry Supinski also contributed valuable records for this story.

In 1991, I wrote to Alice Gawronski after seeing an article in the newspaper about her. Twenty years later, she contacted me and said she was ready to tell her side of the story. The resulting work, "Bad Choices," is my attempt to do just that. I am thankful Alice trusted me with this, and I also thank attorney Joe Hurley for his colorful re-creation of the trial and its aftermath. Author of *I Heard You Paint Houses* and attorney, Charles Brandt deserves my special thanks for providing background on Frank Sheeran and helping me make some sense out of a confusing tale.

"Love, Lies and Lycra Secrets," the last story in the book, was actually my first attempt at publishing a story. My friend Jerry Capone brought a case he had just finished to me with the thought that I could make something out of it. That put me on the long path that led to this book, and for that, I owe Jerry my thanks. I had the incredible opportunity to interview attorneys on both sides of this case, Jerry Capone and Ray Radulski for the defense and Edmond Falgowski and now federal Appellate Court judge Kent Jordan for the prosecution. They were all very helpful and cooperative and deserving of my thanks. The central figure in the story, Maria de Bianchini, wrote a long, detailed and painfully honest letter in response to my questions, and from that, she became the narrator I needed. Her contributions made this story something special.

I want to thank, finally, my wife, Cindy, for her forbearance while I pursued these stories when I should have been pursuing something more lucrative.

1

# BOOKIES, BAWDY HOUSES
# AND CHIEF BLACK

## Vice in Wilmington in the 1930s

*C*hief Black had two rules for Mike McGonegal: don't do business with anyone from out of town and don't do business with anyone who worked in a bank. Unusual restraints for most business pursuits, but to the chief, it was a sensible and practical way to control gambling in Wilmington in the early part of the twentieth century. Today, Mike McGonegal might be referred to as a lottery commissioner, but in his day, his chosen line of work earned him the much more colorful title of "bookie." McGonegal was part of the fabric of bookmaking operations, illegal bars and houses of prostitution, or bawdy houses, that flourished in early twentieth-century Wilmington with the at least tacit approval of George A. Black, the long-term chief of police and superintendent of public safety. In 1936, this understanding between Chief Black and McGonegal and similar arrangements with a madam named Edna and many others around town would come spiraling down, all set in motion because Dewey Bartlett wanted one more drink to top off the night.

Wilmington was a far different place in the years between the world wars than it is today. The city was growing and changing with an influx of immigrant workers that pushed its population up 40 percent to over 100,000 between 1900 and 1940. While in 1914 it was home to 319 manufacturing plants that employed over 15,000 workers in shipyards, tanneries, textile mills and breweries, Wilmington saw a shift in the latter part of this period to a more white-collar employment base. Manufacturing plants had declined by half by 1933, brought on partly by the Great Depression, and were being replaced by the influx of new jobs supporting DuPont, Hercules and Atlas Powder Company. It was a city of stark contrasts. The Internal Revenue Service said in 1927 that Wilmington was the richest city in America per capita, yet in the early 1930s, nearly half of the city's residences had no indoor toilets. There were strong ethnic enclaves of Polish, Irish and Italian immigrants and upper-class neighborhoods with executives working for the chemical companies. Union Park Gardens was built to provide housing for the shipyard workers in this era while Wawaset Park came into being to house executives in a deed-restricted environment.

Wilmington police chief/ superintendent of public safety George A. Black, 1932. *Collections of the Delaware Historical Society.*

Into this mix was added the vice trade, with numbers rackets, speakeasies and houses of prostitution all competing for the illegal dollar. Bill McLaughlin remembered those days. The man who would go on to serve two terms as Wilmington's mayor in the 1970s and '80s grew up on the corner of Fifth and Pine Streets, one of twelve children. He came of age in the 1930s when Wilmington, like the rest of the country, was mired in the Great Depression. "My father lost his job, so I quit school when I was 16," McLaughlin said. "It's amazing the things you did to survive, but that's what you did; you survived."

George Black was a fixture in Wilmington by then. Black was born in Delaware in 1868 and joined the Wilmington Police Department as a patrol officer in 1891, making chief in 1902. From then on, he was the ever-present source of power and influence in the city. Black became superintendent of public safety in 1921 in addition to chief of police when the City of Wilmington merged police and fire administrations. "You have to remember that Chief Black ran a pretty good city, he really did," recalled McLaughlin. "They knew they couldn't stop the corruption, but my god, they wanted to make [Wilmington] decent. This is going to happen anyhow so you might as well have some control over it. And to me it worked pretty well. We didn't have any gangsters here like Philadelphia or New York City had. Chester, they had gangsters, but we didn't have anything like that."

Whether or not Wilmington had gangsters, there was still vice activity during George Black's tenure on the police force, though the reported scope of activity varied greatly depending on the source. The Wilmington police

in those days consisted of a chief, 2 captains and 4 sergeants and a force of about 160 officers, all reporting to the Board of Police Commissioners. "The mayor and council didn't have administrative authority over day-to-day dealings," stated O. Francis Biondi. Biondi was city solicitor for Wilmington under Mayor John Babiarz in 1964 and was primarily responsible for writing the new city charter that year that did away with the board and commissioner system of government. "The council set the tax rates and budgets, but the commissioners ran the departments on a daily basis, controlling hiring and administering the personnel system."

By 1896, Black had risen to sergeant. The chief at the time, John F Dolan, said in his 1897 annual report that "our city has, during the past year, been very free of crime. Very few serious violations of law have occurred. Arrests listed for gambling offenses or policy [numbers] writing were almost nonexistent."

Dolan was succeeded as chief by former sergeant Eugene Massey on August 1, 1900, with Black moving up to captain around the same time. By December 1901, Chief Massey was brought up on charges by the Board of Police Commissioners and a situation in stark contrast to the former chief's annual report began to emerge. Newspaper articles and editorials had been running for several months regarding gambling activities in Wilmington, bringing attention to bear on police officers and commissioners alike. Several officers testified before the commissioners in December 1901 and January 1902 that they were aware of gambling operations but claimed they could not get the chief to issue arrest warrants. Former police commissioner William Pyle stated that he spoke to Chief Massey on several occasions about the gambling activity but was unable to get any action from him. He then went to Captain Black after he was named a state detective. (Black briefly resigned from the Wilmington police force in 1901 but was reinstated as captain again a few weeks later.) Pyle said, "Captain, I cannot get anything done in the policy business. I wish you would take it up....You are under the control of nobody but the attorney general. I said you can suppress it and I want to see it done." Later Pyle testified, "On the following Saturday afternoon after his appointment, which was one week, he [Black] had warrants out for, I think, 7 or 8 persons, 4 of whom he arrested."

State detective Theodore Francis was questioned at length by the commissioners about gambling activities. When asked whether "the town was wide open, was it not?" he answered, "Yes sir. There was no trouble for anyone to play [policy/numbers] who wanted to....I suppose when policy is going full blast about 50–60% of the people play policy." Detective Francis also spoke of meetings with a Samuel Levy of Philadelphia, a policy backer, where Levy offered Detective Francis $100 per month for police protection. At a later meeting, Levy told Detective Francis, "I am willing to pay for protection and won't do business in any city unless I pay for the protection." Francis stated that Levy said the chief (Massey) was a very nice man, but "I can't do anything with this man Black down there. There don't appear to be any way to reach him."

Chief Massey admitted meeting Levy in Philadelphia and at the B&O railway station in Wilmington but made no effort to arrest him for his gambling activities. The testimony most damaging to Chief Massey came from Captain George Black himself. In addition to testifying about attending meetings between Chief Massey and Samuel Levy, Black stated that he was present when Chief Massey opened letters from Levy containing bank notes, which Massey placed in his pocket. "I said it would make trouble sooner or later and advised him not to have anything to do with Levy," Black testified. "He [Massey] said it was not contrary to the rules of the department to take a present and he took this bank note as a present."

Chief Massey denied taking money from Levy but was dismissed from the police force on January 28, 1902, by the Board of Police Commissioners for neglect of duty and conduct unbecoming an officer. On the same day Massey's dismissal made front-page news, another story alongside it trumpeted "Great Police Raid," stating, "Police Captain George Black and a squad of nearly 50 officers last night, on evidence furnished by the Law and Order Society, made a raid on the disorderly houses of the city." Over 20 houses were raided and over 100 arrests were made. The Law and Order Society was a militant organization based in New Jersey and Philadelphia formed to combat the evils of the saloon, prostitution and gambling.

The Wilmington branch of the Law and Order Society brought in its own detectives to find the bawdy houses and illegal bars operating throughout the city. The Reverend Dr. Hahnnd headed up the investigation and had this to say about the results: "In all my experience…I feel sure I have never seen or heard of a more debased condition of affairs anywhere than have existed in Wilmington, not only in relation to the bawdy houses, but also to the illegal sale of liquor." He went on to "extend special compliments to Captain Black for the most excellent manner in which he planned and executed the raid."

Almost immediately, a push was on to name George Black the new chief. Under the headline "Talk of New Chief" was the subheading "Friends of Capt. Black Put Him Forward." In the article, it stated that the friends of Captain Black "claim he is the logical successor as he is the highest Republican officer in the department and should be promoted accordingly." On February 17, 1902, George Black was named Wilmington's chief of police at age thirty-four, the youngest officer above the rank of patrolman.

Black came in riding a reputation as an officer above reproach who was willing to crack down on vice. But some questioned his character. Former chief Massey claimed Black had been caught riding in a carriage on Kennett Pike with a woman who was not his wife and his wife had been sent an anonymous letter about the incident. Massey said Black blamed him for the anonymous letter, which was why he lied about Massey receiving money from Samuel Levy. James Walls, one of the men busted by Captain Black in the gambling raid, signed an affidavit claiming Black was operating under instructions from Samuel Levy in the raid. According to Walls, Levy viewed Walls and his partners as competition and wanted them eliminated. Walls later recanted the affidavit in front of the police commissioners investigating the claim, and Black was vindicated.

# A New Chief

Within months of becoming chief, George Black had his first brush with notoriety, dealing with an event that earned Wilmington a presidential censure. In 1903, the teenaged daughter of the superintendent of the Ferris School was murdered near Prices Corner. A Black farmhand named George White was arrested by Chief Black and sent to the County Workhouse on Greenbank Road. Newspaper headlines like "Fiend Assaults Young Woman" inflamed public opinion. "If a trial is not forthcoming," the minister of Olivet Presbyterian Church at Fourth and Broom Streets, Robert Elwood, harangued a nighttime crowd of three thousand, "then the citizens of the state should arise in their might and execute the criminal, and thus uphold the majesty of the law."

On the night of June 22, 1903, a mob estimated at several thousand people converged on the Workhouse armed with clubs, rifles and, some claim, dynamite, to take the prisoner. As the group approached the prison door, Chief Black and a squad of patrolmen emerged from the prison, and Chief Black told the crowd anyone advancing farther would be shot. This threat was met with jeers, and the crowd, surging forward, forced the officers back inside. "It was decided," said Chief Black to a newspaper reporter

He Always Gets His Man

Cartoon showing Chief Black in action. *Courtesy of Wilmington Police Department Archives.*

the next day, "after a consultation, not to use firearms on the mob, and it is probable that through that decision a great loss of life was avoided." The mob forced their way to the prisoner's cell and removed him to a large field near the alleged crime scene. There, George White was bound hand and foot, thrown on a flaming pyre of straw and fence rails and burned to death. The lynching made national news and shocked President Theodore Roosevelt. Roosevelt took this incident and an attempted lynching in Indiana that same summer as an opportunity to strongly condemn the practice and particularly the "dreaded torture of fire."

In 1911, Chief Black was again in the news, this time over charges leveled by two state representatives that he accepted bribes to allow the opening of a "bawdy house" in Wilmington. These charges, brought at the behest of his former champion, the Law and Order Society, led to a public hearing by a committee set up by the speaker of the State House of Representatives. During the hearing, Black denied there were rules in his administration for bawdy houses, although he acknowledged under former Chief Dolan there was a rule to prevent women from sitting in windows and soliciting business. He also admitted to trying to keep these houses out of the better parts of town, confining them to the slums. "Although the House investigation proved a tremendous sensation, with various ladies of the underworld parading to the Court House, the charges failed to stick. Chief Black was given a clean bill of health and emerged triumphant, more firmly entrenched than ever."

With Chief Black strongly established, anyone wishing to open for business had to deal with him. And there were many in Wilmington who saw the vice trade as a way to make a living. One of them was Mike McGonegal. McGonegal's father, John, had emigrated from Ireland and, by 1888, had established his family in Wilmington, where he worked as a quarryman for Brandywine Granite. His death at age thirty-seven left Mike, his mother and his family without any means of support. As the oldest children, Mike and his twin brother, Phil, went to work at age fourteen as glazers in one of the morocco leather tanneries around Wilmington.

His first love was always sports, and from an early age, he coached baseball and basketball teams on Wilmington's west side, particularly for West End Neighborhood House and St. Ann's Parish. From the early 1900s through the 1930s, the sports stars of west Wilmington all played for Mike McGonegal teams. Players such as Buck Lacey, Buzzie Gillen, Elec Kelleher, Paul Hahn, Tommy Conaty, Paul Chadick, Charlie Noonan and Mike's sons, Jimmy, Mike and Billy, came back year after year to play baseball or basketball for "The Baron." Perhaps this led him into the sports betting arena and ultimately to running a numbers bank, but by his early twenties, he had left the tanneries and was working on his own. By the 1930s, he reportedly had the biggest book on the city's west side. Even then, his public persona was still in the sports arena, coaching teams and organizing sports leagues. At his death, a newspaper columnist called him "one of the most colorful figures in Delaware sports circles. McGonegal was regarded as one of the greatest promoters of amateur athletics Wilmington has ever seen."

Joe Jamison grew up in Wilmington in those days and remembered the numbers trade. "Everybody played the numbers and they paid off when your number hit. It was a real business and it never hurt anybody." Mike McGonegal was a prominent person on Wilmington's west side, doing everything from running his numbers bank to coaching his basketball and baseball teams and bailing those in need out of jail. "Anybody who needed money went to him," recalled Jamison. "If people had ever paid him back, he'd have died a millionaire."

In the Wilmington city directories, Mike McGonegal was listed variously as the operator of a cigar store or as a salesman. Once, a door-to-door surveyor for the directories commented on the fact that he always seemed to have a new Studebaker. Mike McGonegal told him that he sold them for a living, so for the next few years, the directories dutifully listed him as a Studebaker salesman. He was not the only one in town, though, to give disingenuous answers to a surveyor. One Edna Powell was listed as the widow of William Powell, at 811 North Tatnall Street, with no occupation claimed. However, her husband was far from deceased and the phone number for that address was listed for her "office."

The 1920s ushered in Prohibition, and Wilmington, like other cities, had its share of speakeasies, houses where illegal liquor sales took place on a regular basis. In 1924, Edna Powell opened a speakeasy one block west of the Woman's Christian Temperance Union and Anti-Saloon League headquarters, on the second and third floors of 211 West Eighth Street. By 1928, she had a disorderly house, or house of prostitution, at the same address, and by 1930, she had moved operations around the corner to 811 Tatnall Street. "Tatnall Street was known as the 'tenderloin district,'" related Tom Monahan, a twenty-year veteran of the Wilmington police force and its unofficial historian. "That was the same name they had for it in every city."

Bill McLaughlin remembered Edna Powell's establishment from his teenage years: "I remember we were eighteen years old, and for after-hours drinking you knew where to go. We finally got a group of us together and walked into Edna Powell's, and they served us. God, that was great. It was just a house with a big parlor, and you'd sit around and drink, just like you were visiting. They'd sell you a bottle of beer for a quarter."

Longtime Wilmington newspaper reporter and columnist Bill Frank wrote a column for the *News-Journal* in 1973, titled "Bawds and Police," in which he described with a great degree of familiarity the "notorious fancy houses that once operated with varying degrees of finesse and decorum." Frank listed a half dozen addresses in downtown Wilmington as the best-known "sporting houses" and that the going rate for female companionship was two dollars. Extras called for a five-dollar tab.

Edna Powell mugshot, 1936. *Courtesy of Wilmington Police Department Archives.*

*The average bawdy house—at least in Wilmington—was not a boisterous place. With few exceptions, decorum was always maintained. And the madam always sought to protect their gentlemen friends from the police and, if need be, those friends' identities.*

*The most dignified of all was 602 French Street, reigned over by a matronly type known to her clientele as Mom. She once said she'd known two generations of customers and liked them all....*

*The most interesting house was Edna Powell's....It was a good example of a combination drinking and sex operation....Edna herself was picturesque, an excellent conversationalist, and attractive in a Mae West sort of way when she bothered to doll up. On a Saturday night, customers included many prominent men about town, seeking booze rather than broads....At times a client would find himself in the parlor more than an hour without catching a glimpse of a woman....If he'd like companionship, he'd give Edna a strong hint and she'd walk over to the stairway leading to the second floor to sing out "Customers, girls." Several girls in lounging pajamas would appear. This meant the customer bought rounds of drinks before disappearing upstairs with one of the service staff.*

One year after Edna Powell opened her first speakeasy, Chief Black's son George Black Jr. was sworn in as a Wilmington police officer on his twenty-first birthday. By 1928, he had made sergeant and quickly rose to lieutenant and captain. Though he physically resembled his father, the chief, Young George, as he was called, was a very different person. "He was just a no-gooder, that's what he was," recalled Bill McLaughlin. "We'd be shooting craps at Fifth and Spruce by Allied Kid [a leather tannery]. We were just kids, about fourteen to fifteen years old. He'd let us get started and then chase us away with the money laying on the ground. He'd just pick up the money and walk away."

GEORGE A. BLACK
*Captain of Traffic*

Captain George Black, son of Chief Black. *Courtesy of Wilmington Police Department Archives.*

Jane Riley Jones also remembered Young George Black. "He was sarcastic and surly. It was like he was running the place." When she was a child, Jane's parents' house on Linden Street near St. Hedwig's Church in the Hedgeville section of Wilmington was used by Mike McGonegal to collect and record bets on horse races and the numbers. One of Mike's men was Tim Quill, who sometimes worked out of the Linden Street house to take bets on the horses. His son Leonard recalled how his father would collect the bets: "He'd get a loaf of bread and hollow it out, then when he'd collect the bets, he'd stick the slips in the loaf of bread. If he was stopped by the cops all they'd see was the bread."

# DEATH IN A BAWDY HOUSE

In the early morning of March 29, 1936, Dewey Bartlett and his friend Joseph Coombs were drinking at another speakeasy and decided to get a night cap at Edna Powell's establishment on Tatnall Street. Entering by the alley passage to the rear bar room, Coombs ordered whiskey for himself, Barlett and two other friends in the bar. Working at the bar was Edna Powell's supposedly deceased ex-husband, William, along with their son, Charles, and her current boyfriend, Harold Witsil. Bartlett suggested Coombs set up the house, but when it came time to pay, Coombs said he'd only pay for four drinks instead of eight. "Coombs and father started arguing over drinks," Edna Powell's twenty-six-year-old son, Charles Powell, would later testify. "I asked father to cut it out, but he said, 'I know this fellow and he's no good.' As I started back of the bar again, Bartlett swung at me and I swung at him. I saw my father strike Coombs twice in the face with his fist, he knocked Coombs back a little distance." Harold Witsil then struck Bartlett. "I saw Witsil hit Dewey Bartlett with his right fist, then Witsil turned away and I saw Bartlett sink downward and fall face down on the floor." Edna Powell hit Coombs with a smoking stand when he was on his way out the door.

The ruckus lasted only moments, but at the end, Bartlett lay still in a heap on the floor. Witsil threw cold water on his face, but that failed to revive him. Earl "Kid" Johnson, a former prizefighter who worked as a bouncer at Powell's, was in the other room asleep when the fight broke out. He came into the barroom, looked down at Bartlett and said, "That man is dead." Bartlett was left on the floor while a doctor was called and later pronounced him dead on the scene. "I didn't know I hit him as hard as I did," exclaimed Witsil later under police interrogation. Dewey Bartlett, a thirty-eight-year-old father of six, died of a broken neck and a fractured skull over a two-dollar bar bill.

The police rounded up nine people and questioned them about the crime for over forty hours straight, with Superintendent Black personally supervising the interrogations. At first, Charles and William Powell and Witsil concocted a story about the two friends, Coombs and Bartlett, having the argument and blaming Coombs for the assault.

On April 2, while they were all still in custody, Edna Powell visited her ex-husband, William Powell, with a proposition. "She said, 'Bill, why don't you take the rap?'" according to William Powell. "'I said, who me?' and she said, 'Wait, let me tell you. You know Harold [Witsil] is a high degree Mason and his people is worth a lot of money…he will get out of it.' I said, 'I am not going to take no rap for something I didn't do.' She said, 'If you don't [their son] Charles is.'" Instead, William Powell turned state's evidence and identified Witsil as the assailant.

A New Castle County grand jury indicted Witsil for manslaughter in May, while charging Edna Powell; her son, Charles; her former husband, William; and two other employees of Powell's with conspiracy to obstruct justice. The prosecuting attorney at the trial, Attorney General P. Warren Green, said Powell's establishment was "a joint where no decent, respectable person would be seen," describing the barred windows, the signal system and strong-arm methods used to beat the price of drinks out of the customers.

Harold Witsil mugshot, 1936. *Courtesy of Wilmington Police Department Archives.*

On May 1, 1936, at Wilmington's first-annual police dinner, held at the Hotel DuPont, a letter was read from J. Edgar Hoover, head of the Federal Bureau of Investigation, praising the work of Superintendent George Black. In his letter, Hoover claimed, "Mr. Black possesses not only a national but an international reputation for integrity and efficiency. He combines the best qualities and characteristics of the old and new law enforcement executives." Complimenting Black on his "unblemished integrity," Hoover went on to say, "I have availed myself of the opportunity of often calling upon him for advice and assistance." Within a few months, J. Edgar Hoover and his FBI would play a far different role in Chief Black's career.

On May 20, 1936, Harold Witsil was found guilty of manslaughter and sentenced to two years in prison. The next day, the State Liquor Commission banned the sale of liquor to all those involved in the case. Attorney General Green, though, was much more interested in what Edna Powell and her associates knew about the activities of Chief Black and Young George Black than in the Bartlett case. According to Edna Powell, when she was arrested at the time of the murder, "they [Attorney General Green and Lieutenant James C. Riley] kept me for a couple of days without anything to eat and tried to get me to say that I paid Supt. Black and Capt. Black and other members of the Department [for protection]."

There had been suspicions by Public Safety Board members about the activities of the Blacks before, including alleged payments from bookies, but no action had been taken. Tom Monahan was familiar with the allegations about Chief Black. "One of the things I'm pretty sure [Chief] Black was in to was the restaurant at 11th and Market Street," Monahan said. "They supplied the prisoner meals and Black got a kickback on that. That was called 'clean' corruption in those days. There was clean money and dirty money, but it's a slippery slope."

Perhaps the Attorney General's office and the Public Safety Board were reflecting a lower tolerance for this type of activity by a changing Wilmington demographic, with white-collar executives replacing the predominant blue-collar working population. Or perhaps Captain Black's transgressions had become so blatant that they could no longer be ignored. In either case, Attorney General Green had an opportunity to crack down on corrupt practices in Wilmington.

A crackdown on corruption in Wilmington by Attorney General Green would need a break, and the newly charged Edna Powell was a logical place to start applying pressure for information. Powell was not going to be a pushover for law enforcement, however, and let it be known that she had ammunition to use. As she told her associate, Shelley Fisher, if Green and Chief Black did not leave her alone, she was going to tell (former Public Safety Board member and New Castle County Republican Party chair) V. Wirt Willis a story that would blow the lid off.

Attorney General Green kept the pressure on Edna Powell with prosecutions for numerous crimes. She was subsequently convicted of conspiracy to falsely accuse an innocent man, assault and battery on Joseph Coombs, selling intoxicating liquor without a license and keeping a house of prostitution. At midsummer she was still out of prison appealing her sentences, but after many weeks, she yielded to the pressure and decided to talk. On July 24, 1936, she made the first of two affidavits to the attorney general. By August 7, her ex-husband, William; her son, Charles; and her boyfriend, Harold Witsil, had also filed affidavits, giving the attorney general and the Public Safety Board what they needed to act. The Board of Directors of the Public Safety Department quietly assigned two officers, Lieutenant James C. Riley and Detective Robert Wallace, to investigate alleged misconduct by police officials.

Chief Black was informed that officers Riley and Wallace were being removed from his supervision and were instructed to report only to the city solicitor and the directors of Public Safety. Also, on August 4, 1936, the board specifically ordered Superintendent Black to immediately close all houses of prostitution, gambling houses, illegal bars and numbers banks in Wilmington. State attorney general P. Warren Green hired the William J. Burns detective agency to make its own investigation of operations in Wilmington. The private detectives would report to Green and City Solicitor James R. Morford.

Things did not remain quiet for long, and within a week of giving her first affidavit, Edna Powell was front-page news. Word leaked to the press that she had made a statement to the attorney general about how she was able to operate her illegal establishment and that the attorney general had turned the statement over to the public safety board. No details of the charges were made public, but rumors about police payoffs were given play. Superintendent Black said this was the first he had heard about the Powell accusations and refused other comment. "The rumors going around at present put every member of the force under suspicion," one policeman was quoted as saying. Edna Powell was sought out by reporters but refused to discuss the case. "Puffing a cigarette nervously she gave the same answer, 'I have no comment to make' to every question."

"They didn't have internal affairs back then," recalled twenty-six-year Wilmington police veteran Kevin Quinn. Quinn's mother, Kitty Riley Quinn, was the oldest of six children of Lieutenant James C. Riley, better known as Curt. Kevin Quinn remembers the stories of his grandfather when he was growing up in Wilmington and had a chance to read Curt Riley's memoirs before they were destroyed in a flood. "My grandfather in his younger days was a bare-knuckle prize fighter. He could fight. He wasn't the biggest man in the world, but he had huge hands and could really box." Curt Riley joined the force in 1910 and by 1936 was a detective lieutenant.

Also working the case with the attorney general and City Solicitor James Morford was a young assistant city solicitor named Thomas Herlihy Jr., a fellow member with Chief Black of DuPont Lodge No.29, Free and Accepted Masons. His son Tom III, born the same year as the investigation, knows from his father's recollections that this was an exceptionally tense time for his family. His father was concerned about possible reprisals against himself and his family.

By August 1, the rumors were becoming even more lurid. "Federal agents are reported to have been investigating the Powell place since her last arrest

JAMES C. RILEY
Lieutenant of Detectives

Lieutenant James C. Riley.
*Courtesy of Wilmington Police Department Archives.*

in an effort to discover if it had any connection with an eastern white slave circle," the *Wilmington Morning News* breathlessly reported. "She is said to have made her statement after being pressed by them [federal agents]." In fact, on August 7, Attorney General Green did contact the FBI Philadelphia office, which replied that it was investigating neither Edna Powell's allegations nor irregularities in the Wilmington Police Department.

## THE CHIEF FIGHTS BACK

Members of the police department began a counteroffensive even though no one had been publicly accused of anything yet. The newspapers began to report unnamed officers questioning the integrity of the supposed charges by Edna Powell. "Considering the fact that her place has been raided from time to time… some of the police, they said, naturally must have incurred her antagonism with the result that innocent men may be among those she accused," said one news story. Other police were reported to have consulted an attorney and were prepared to take legal action in the event of unsubstantiated charges. Comparisons were made to the 1911 case against then-chief Black, who was said to have been the victim of a frame-up at the time and was exonerated of all charges. The investigation "won't amount to a row of pins," a "high official who has been figured in the case prominently thus far, has been prompted to remark." The entire probe will "collapse when accused members of the force refute Mrs. Powell's condemnations."

Chief Black began a very public display of enforcing the board's order to close all of the illegal gambling operations, speakeasies and bawdy houses. "67 Seized in Raids as Police Launch City-Wide Cleanup," proclaimed the newspaper headlines on August 7. "Police battered in doors, tore down barred windows and forced their way into a score of alleged gambling and liquor centers in a general roundup" as a strike force of nineteen officers struck a dozen addresses simultaneously. Buried in the back of the news story was the following passage: "The successful raids yesterday were only a small part of the actual number made by the police and detectives. In many cases they found the supposed 'bookie joints' locked tightly with no sign of life and every indication that the place had been vacated. In other instances they were met by the proprietor who greeted them politely and invited them to step in and look around. In which case they found the place deserted with no sign that a bet had ever been placed there."

By August 16, the headline was "Vice, Gambling at Lowest Ebb Here, Police Say," and then the story disappeared from the public's view. Behind the scenes, though, the investigation was just getting underway as Lieutenant Riley and Detective Wallace undertook their assignment from the Public Safety Board.

As Riley and Wallace began their investigation, the reach of Chief Black and his son Captain Black soon became apparent. Within a week, Riley had reported that two unnamed individuals had approached him and asked that he not "hunt up" any evidence against the Blacks other than what City Solicitor Morford had specifically requested. Riley told them he had not asked for this assignment but had to follow through with it. "I don't think my grandfather had any real problems with Chief Black," said Kevin Quinn. "He had major problems with Capt. Black. He despised him. They kind of tolerated each other and stayed out of each other's way."

In August, Chief Black asked Detective William Hynson about the whereabouts of Riley and Wallace and suggested they should be followed to see where they went and what they were doing. Unsuccessful in getting a fellow police officers to help, Chief Black then reached outside the force to a trusted associate. On September 14, Detective Robert Wallace was visited at home at 1300 North Scott Street by Dominic Nardo, a barber by profession, who told Wallace he was sent by Chief Black, who wanted to know what he and Lieutenant Riley had found, in particular what derogatory information they had on the chief. Detective Wallace wouldn't disclose anything about the investigation.

Fifty years after these events, Tom Monahan sat down with Dominic Nardo. "He did have a barbershop just off Market Street. He was legitimately a barber, but his main business was that of a bookie…and an enforcer. Talking to him [Nardo], you felt like you were in a movie. He had this heavy Italian accent, and he wouldn't let us record the conversation, but he agreed to be very candid. 'Look,' he said, 'Chief Black was my friend. That boy [Captain Black] was a son of a bitch, but Chief Black was my friend.'"

Potential witnesses in the case were being subjected to threats and intimidation. One, a bookmaker, told the investigating officers that he had been paying Captain Black $20 a month by mailing the money to Captain

Black's home. The witness was later visited by two men who said they had been told that the bookmaker was about to "squeal." Now the witness was afraid to talk. He had been willing to testify against Captain Black if the pending case against him was dropped, but intermediaries for Black were offering to cover the cost of his fine ($400) and arrange for his jail sentence to be dropped. City Solicitor Morford noted that this witness now "will not talk."

Edna Powell was still out on appeal in October and coming under increasing pressure from both Chief Black and Attorney General Green. One of the private detectives spoke with a person named Harvey, who ran a speakeasy at 105 West Eighth Street. Harvey had spoken to Edna Powell, and she was mad. According to Harvey, Edna said, "I have plenty to holler about after the way I paid off and now the cops are trying to ride me. Why don't they try and find out how some others get their bankroll, and if they think they are scaring me, they are badly mistaken because certain people from the [news]paper have been to see me and offered me $5,000 for a copy of the report I turned over, so if I don't come out on top, I sure will give this out so it can be published. They think just because my boyfriend [Witsil] is doing two years for that murder, they have me frightened, but I refuse to be scared."

On October 19, 1936, Edna was visited by the operator of another disorderly house at 801 Tatnall Street. She suggested Edna go see Superintendent Black and Bill Warren, the "Fishman" (Warren ran a fish store on King Street), who might help her out of her trouble. Edna set up a meeting for October 22 with Bill Warren at 801 Tatnall Street. Warren told Edna that if she wrote Superintendent Black a letter telling him what Attorney General Green, City Solicitor Morford, Lieutenant Riley and officer Wallace were doing in the investigation, Black would get her out of all her trouble. Warren told her that Wallace, Riley, Morford and Green were no friends of hers and that they were using her. At Warren's direction, she wrote the letter to Black, signed it E.P. and sent it by taxi to Black's office in the public building in the 1000 block of King Street.

The pressure on the investigating officers in this case was also reaching a new level. Curt Riley and his family lived just off of Washington Street and Concord Avenue, and the younger children walked to school each day. "The kids would be coming home from school and a guy gave them a letter, telling them to give it to their mother," related Kevin Quinn. "People didn't mess with Curt Riley, not physically. So, the thing to do was to get to his children. The letter had threats against his wife and children, not him."

This was not the only threatening letter to be delivered. Starting in October 1936, anonymous letters "of a threatening and defamatory nature" were sent to two current and one former director of public safety, plus four anonymous letters to the two investigating officers. The threats particularly centered on Lieutenant Riley, whose family received three letters over four weeks that were later described as "obscene, lewd, scurrilous, defamatory and threatening, and containing indecent and profane language."

Kevin Quinn confirmed the problems encountered by his grandfather Lieutenant Riley in his investigation of his fellow officers. "Captain Black was a powerful figure in the department. My grandfather got the cold shoulder from his fellow officers. He got pretty bad treatment until this thing finally went down."

On November 14, 1936, Detective Wallace traveled to Washington, D.C., with copies of seven of the anonymous letters, headed for the Federal Bureau of Investigation. There he conferred with J. Edgar Hoover and submitted the letters along with handwriting samples of several suspects, including Captain Black, to the FBI's technical lab for examination. By November 17, the FBI had sent its report on the handwriting analysis back to Wilmington, but Hoover decided to direct the report to Chief Black instead of forwarding it to the city solicitor or the investigating officers. Chief Black held on to the report and began correspondence with his old friend the FBI director.

Chief Black wrote to Hoover:

> You are no doubt aware of the fact that there has been a very secret investigation conducted during the past three or four months by City Solicitor James R. Morford....This has placed all members of our department on what we may justly term 'The Spot' and has caused considerable feeling among the members towards certain ones, especially the Detectives making the investigation, which was to be expected. The result no doubt has been that certain members have written letters which evidently have been submitted to your department for investigation....I am very much surprised and shocked to know that they have suspected my son, Captain George A. Black, who has positively denied to me that he has any knowledge whatever concerning these letters, and I will certainly consider it a very personal favor if you can advise me just what it is all about and what they are trying to accuse my son of doing.

On November 23, 1936, Hoover wrote back to Black, saying, "My dear Superintendent, I certainly am exceedingly concerned that you should be worried in any manner, directly or indirectly, by any development involving your son. So far as this bureau is concerned, I want to assure you that we have no information or interest in this investigation." Hoover went on to relate the visit from Officer Robert Wallace and the steps the bureau had taken regarding the anonymous letters.

City Solicitor Morford was livid when he discovered Hoover's actions. As he wrote to Public Safety Board president Schutt on November 30, "The Department of Justice [FBI], either through a very stupid mistake or deliverately [sic] sent their preliminary report to Supt. Black instead of me. Chief Black has never turned the copy over to me or so far as I know taken any steps to supply the Department of Investigation with the additional information requested. As soon as I found out what had been done I demanded a copy of the letter from Hoover to Black."

Thomas Herlihy's son Jerome O. Herlihy recalled his father's opinion of J. Edgar Hoover's actions: "He blew the investigation." That the target of the investigation was contacted by the FBI director with evidence was "outside of protocol."

When the FBI report finally reached the detectives and city solicitor, they saw it confirmed the opinions of two handwriting experts hired by the attorney general: all of the anonymous letters had in fact been written by Captain Black. With the confidentiality of the investigation blown by the FBI director, the detectives and attorney general needed to bring the case forward. Thirty-eight subpoenas were immediately issued to cops and underworld figures alike to compel testimony about police corruption.

On December 1, 1936, fifteen charges against Superintendent George Black and sixteen against his son Captain George A. Black were filed by City Solicitor James R. Morford at an executive meeting of the directors of the Department of Public Safety, with a trial board scheduled three days hence. The charges painted a picture of a police department on the take and out of the control of the superintendent. Captain Black was portrayed as a venal and bullying figure, shaking down the bookies and bootleggers for cash, selling police protection to bawdy houses. He was not alone, as thirty officers were named by Edna Powell and her associates in their affidavits. As for Chief Black, charges were mainly of incompetence, willful neglect and conduct subversive of good order and discipline. He was also charged with willful disobedience to orders and neglect of duty regarding his failure to close gambling houses and houses of prostitution.

"All of us knew that [police taking payoffs] was going on," recalled Bill McLaughlin. "We could see sometimes policemen taking these envelopes. Somebody'd walk out and hand them something. It was just taken for granted that was the price of doing business."

## DAMNING TESTIMONY

Edna Powell was the star witness at the trial board on December 4, 1936. By this time, she was serving her sentence at the women's prison on Greenbank Road near the County Workhouse. Her story detailed not just payoffs but also how elements of the police department controlled the illegal trade in Wilmington, from who could open up shop to who got tipped off about pending raids. "I got pinched on March 22, 1930 at 811 Tatnall St.," stated Edna Powell in her deposition, "and it was after that I started to pay for protection."

The payoffs for police protection went back five or six years, and the infrequent raids on her establishment were always preceded by a telephone call from a police source tipping her off. (The signal was three phone calls in a row with no answer.) "The phone call would come in to the Powells that the police were on their way to raid," according to Monahan. "All the girls would go up to the Barn Door [restaurant up the street] except for one. Everyone had to have their turn once a month getting arrested."

The payments for police protection had its own set of standards and practices. "The rule was that we would have to take care of the officers Easter, vacation, Thanksgiving, Christmas, and the sergeants and detectives all in between," said Edna Powell in her deposition. "In my judgment I have paid between $3,000 and $4,000 over six years of time. I paid out about $700 last Christmas to the police officers. It kept me broke paying the officers. I had to stay open all night in order to get enough money to pay them." Those officers on the take knew better than to bite the hand feeding them. "About 4 or 5 years ago I was supposed to be raided one night," testified Edna Powell. "The detective called and told me I was going to get raided, and I told him that this was soldiers pay day. He told me he would postpone it until tomorrow which was done. The next day I was raided."

Edna Powell also testified about another prostitution house operator receiving a letter from the superintendent (George Black Sr.) telling her she must vacate the premises immediately. Powell made arrangements for her to pay protection and she had been making payments ever since. She named names of patrolmen, sergeants and officers all the way to Captain Black himself taking cash payments. She also named other establishments throughout downtown and how the operators shared complaints about cops demanding payments. "It got so bad in the summer of 1934 that [another prostitution house operator] and I decided to go to Atlantic City to stay for 3 weeks to get away from the cops."

After the Bartlett murder, Lieutenant Riley had ordered Powell to close her disorderly house at 811 Tatnall Street. A few weeks later, she approached Captain Black about permission to reopen. "I told him I didn't intend to open up wide but enough to make expenses," stated Edna Powell. "Black told me to go ahead on his say so, and if he heard anything that it was not alright he would call me and let me know."

Harold Witsil also testified about the payoffs, detailing the schedule for the Christmas payoffs to as many as thirty officers. Patrolmen got five dollars, sergeants ten dollars, captains twenty and Captain Black his usual twenty-five. No mention was made of a payoff to Chief Black. Other testimony told of payments to Captain Black from ten to fifteen dollars a month for protection of a bootlegging operation to fifteen dollars a week to protect operations of a disorderly house. Several operators of bawdy houses thought Attorney General Green was in on the rackets and would shut the investigation down.

A succession of police officers and private citizens testified about seeing Captain Black meeting with bookies and bootleggers over the last several years, in some cases taking payments of money and liquor. One person testified that she saw a bootlegger drive slowly by Captain Black's car, reach out an arm with a paper in it, hand it to Captain Black and drive away. A Detective Cook testified he had arrested a local bootlegger, who was then ordered released by superior officers, only to be rearrested on direct orders of the Public Safety directors. Chief Black later came into the detective bureau and told Detective Cook that he had put him in the detective bureau and that he'd put him out.

Captain Black was hardly subtle. One person testified Captain Black stopped his auto outside a known horse race betting parlor at Eighth and Thornton Streets. Black blew his horn repeatedly for ten to fifteen minutes, attracting considerable attention from the neighborhood. "No one appeared," he said, and Black drove off "as though he would rip the gears off his car." A short time later, the betting parlor was raided by police led by Captain Black.

Sergeant Wadman testified that last June that he and his partner saw Captain Black's car stopped across Linden Street from an automobile and Black was standing next to the vehicle, talking to the driver. When Captain Black saw Sergeant Wadman's patrol car, he got back in his car and hurried away. They pursued the other car and caught up to it at South Clayton and Chestnut Streets. They identified the driver of the other car as "Mike McGonigle [sic]," a bookmaker. According to the officers, McGonegal looked at them and laughed. This clearly was not someone who would cooperate in the investigation.

THE WILMINGTON POLICE BAND — 1936
CAPTAIN GEORGE A. BLACK, *Director*

Wilmington Police Department band. Captain George Black, leader. *Courtesy of Wilmington Police Department Archives.*

No evidence was presented that alleged any payoffs from McGonegal to Captain Black. Even so, it's likely Mike McGonegal was paying for protection. Patrolman James Wilson reported that "every other Monday Capt. Black would meet Mike McGonegil [*sic*], well known bookmaker, in front of Bayard Junior High School on S. Clayton Street." Jane Riley Jones remembers of Captain Black, "Oh, yeah, he was collecting from everybody."

The detective agency hired by the attorney general provided more detail about the criminal activity going on. One private detective said he kept watch on a dozen disorderly houses in Wilmington and found they were still in operation after the general order to close all of them had been issued. In Harvey's at 105 West Eighth Street, private detective Albert Hart observed "young high school couples retiring to the back room while other couples waited in the combination kitchen barroom. They chatted freely…of school affairs while frequenting the sordid resort….The high school students patronized the place particularly on Saturday nights. Their school lessons usually were the topic of conversations between drinks and trips to the bedroom with their partners." Another private detective said he was assured by a disorderly house proprietor that he didn't need to worry, because he was "taking care of the cops." The houses were scattered throughout the downtown, from Second and Adams, 502 Orange and 802 Orange to 602 French and 302 East Second Street. Some of the houses were "chain houses" owned by the same operator, where the women would stay only a week before moving on to the next house.

The testimony of Herman Pontesoff demonstrated the control exerted by the Blacks and the lengths they would go to protect their operation. Pontesoff, better known as Curly, ran a numbers bank in Newark, New Jersey, and wanted to open for business in Wilmington. Pontesoff approached Chief Black through an intermediary, a city employee in the Health Department and bridge tender for the Washington Street Bridge. The intermediary went to the chief and said a man from New Jersey (Pontesoff) wanted to open a numbers game in Wilmington and asked the chief's opinion. Chief Black said he didn't have any objections. The intermediary later arranged a meeting between Pontessof and Captain Black, who was paid $100 and said everything would be alright.

Pontesoff was supposed to testify before the trial board on Friday, December 4, 1936, but was waylaid. Around 1:00 a.m. the night before his testimony, several armed men, possibly including Nardo, approached him leaving a restaurant near the Hotel DuPont. "As he left a man walked behind him and 'shoved a pistol into his back' the investigator stated. Pontesoff was ordered into a machine parked at the curb and was threatened with death if he didn't leave the city." The gunmen drove him to the bus station, where he was put on a bus to Philadelphia. It wasn't until several hours later that the city solicitor was able to reach Pontesoff and persuade him to return to Wilmington with a promise of police protection, provided by Lieutenant Riley.

Taken as a whole, the testimony against Captain Black was damning, with direct evidence of demanding and taking payoffs. There was much less direct evidence against his father's actions, but it was clear what Chief Black permitted on his watch. Vice, in the form of gambling, bootlegging and prostitution was allowed to operate freely as long as the permission of the chief was obtained. Perhaps the chief was just trying to control what he couldn't eliminate, but his son had taken it to a new level. Now police protection was for sale and everyone had to pay to play.

Was the chief himself in on the take? No one knew or no one would tell. Jerome Herlihy had no doubts concerning his father's opinion: "Chief Black was corrupt." In a letter from City Solicitor Morford to the collector of internal revenue for the State of Delaware on December 9, 1936, Morford admitted, "There is no direct evidence concerning the receipt of any money by Supt. Black." Morford went on to say, though, "Frequent rumors came to my attention of bank accounts in other cities," such as Pennsgrove and Camden, New Jersey and Baltimore. "Supt. Black volunteered that he had $10,000 in cash at Artisan's Bank, $20,000 at WSFS….Throughout the investigation it was repeatedly asserted that both of the above-named persons [Superintendent Black and Captain Black] were independently wealthy."

"The gist of my grandfather's investigation from reading his memoirs was that Chief Black was not a crook, he was not taking money directly," recalls Kevin Quinn. "His son was totally corrupt. He had his posse in the police department that were doing collections."

After two days of testimony by the prosecution, neither Black chose to put up a defense. The board refused Captain Black's resignation and dismissed him instead. Chief Black was allowed to resign but was denied any pension benefits. For the man acknowledged as the father of Wilmington's police pension system, this was a demeaning blow.

On his resignation, George A. Black made a statement through his attorney, Joseph A.L. Errigo:

> *I deny each one of the 21 charges as presented by the city solicitor. I know that I am not guilty of the violations with which I have been charged.*
>
> *I have resigned because I didn't care to continue the battle. I have no complaint to make against anyone. I have waived my rights to my pension because of the precarious condition of the fund. I realize that if I were to demand my pension, many widows and orphans would be denied their livelihood. In making this decision my thoughts were not for myself, but for my fellow citizens.*

The following month Edna Powell and Harold Witsil were back before the trial board testifying about other officers caught up in the scheme. Another captain was charged with taking money for police protection and tipping off Edna Powell about raids, plus other lesser charges. Two sergeants and a patrol officer were charged with similar offenses, including ordering Edna Powell to deliver a few cases of beer to the police station. One officer testified that on several occasions his sergeant gave him lists of places to be raided in connection with the numbers racket and told him to telephone the operator of the numbers bank. These four officers were also dismissed from the force, and twenty others were disciplined by demotions or fines.

Curly Pontesoff did not come away empty-handed from his cooperation with the investigation. On hotel stationary from Newark, New Jersey, Pontesoff wrote City Solicitor Morford asking for reimbursement for his travel expenses to Wilmington and for a $100 fine he had paid while supposedly getting protection from the Blacks. Morford approved a payment from the city coffers to Pontesoff for $132.50.

A startling fact looking back on this event was that no police officer was arrested or charged with a crime as a result of this investigation. Perhaps an indication of the public attitude was the editorial in the *Wilmington Morning News* as this scandal came to a conclusion. Titled "Commendable Service," the editorial praised the directors of Public Safety for the "dignified, business-like manner in which they were conducting their inquiry into charges of laxity in the police department....There will be many persons to regret this outcome, but the justice of it must be apparent....Charges are to be preferred against policemen growing out of the looseness in law enforcement and tolerance of illicit business uncovered."

Perhaps the *Sunday Morning Star*'s editorial best summed up public opinion. "We know that whenever a large number of people live in a community there will be gambling, sexual vice, violations of the liquor regulations and similar infractions of the law. But so long as those things are not tolerated in a way to offend the sense of decency of the general public or of citizens not concerned in the offenses we are disposed not to be too critical. There is, of course, a distinct difference between *laissez faire* within certain limits, and the acceptance of or imposition of graft to permit evil things to be done."

Monahan did give Chief Black credit for many innovations. "Black did a lot of good things. He was very forward-thinking in a lot of ways. Wilmington started hiring the first black cops in the 1920s. He initiated the first police academy in the state of Delaware. They hired matrons, women as sworn officers, long before anybody else even thought of it, to try to provide more humane treatment for female prisoners."

The other side of Chief Black was ever present, though. "They expected a certain level of corruption and it was not unusual for the chief to be skimming prisoner meal money, no big deal," says Monahan. "But his son was his true, true downfall."

# EPILOGUE

On March 9, 1937, a jury found Dominic Nardo guilty of attempting to obstruct public justice in a case called "an outgrowth of allegations made in the recent police investigation and trials." The jury recommended mercy.

In April 1937, Edna Powell's attorney petitioned the attorney general and the Board of Pardons to give favorable consideration to her application for pardon or commutation of her sentence. She had been sentenced in October 1936 for conspiracy in the Bartlett manslaughter case to eighteen months in prison, plus in separate trials to three additional months for selling intoxicating liquor and another year for keeping a house of prostitution. Trumpeting her role in the police scandal, the petition stated, "It was because of her evidence and testimony that a thorough investigation was completed which resulted in the complete reformation and reorganization of the Police Bureau of the City of Wilmington. The revelation of graft, dishonesty and corruption in the Police Bureau is unquestionably of great value to the City and State for which some consideration should be given to the person responsible for such disclosure." The petition also stated that "she is repentant and remorseful for a past which she hopes to completely blot from her life. She intends to enter upon a new life of decency and self-respect."

In July 1937, former captain George Black Jr. died of pneumonia at thirty-three years of age. At the time, he was a patient at the State Hospital at Farnhurst being treated for alcoholism. He left behind a wife and two sons.

Andrew J. Kavanaugh was brought in by the public safety directors to make a study of the police and fire departments in December 1937. Kavanaugh, a former chief of police for Rochester, New York, who, as president of the International Association of Chiefs of Police, helped establish the National Police Academy, accepted the superintendency of Wilmington's Department of Public Safety in January 1938.

On January 8, 1938, it was reported that Mayor Walter W. Bacon and the entire city council inspected the Police and Fire Bureaus at the invitation of the Public Safety Board president Harold Schutt. The newspaper reported, "It was the first inspection of the department's two divisions—police and fire—by Council as a body in nearly two decades." The introduction of an outsider to the superintendent's job and the direct involvement of the mayor and council into the operation of the public safety departments as a result of the recent scandals began the erosion of autonomy by the Public Safety Commission, culminating years later in the elimination of the commission form of governance.

St. Ann's baseball team, City League Champs, 1938. Coach Mike McGonegal, author's grandfather (standing far left) and his sons Jim McGonegal (*kneeling second from left*) and Mike Jr. (*kneeling far right*). *Author's collection.*

Mike McGonegal was never called before the Public Safety Board, nor was he prosecuted for his illegal activities. He continued coaching baseball and basketball teams for St. Ann's, with his baseball team winning the City Baseball League championship in 1937, 1938 and 1939. On December 7, 1940, he died at the age of fifty-five, leaving his wife, a daughter and four sons. Wilmington sportswriter Dick Rinard in his column Calling the Turn had this to say about Mike McGonegal's passing: "Whether one liked him or not, no one can deny that Mike McGonegal was one of the most dominant figures in Wilmington sports circles. The fiery Irishman will be missed by all. It will be many a year until another Mike McGonegal comes along with all his color and gusto. For all of us who knew him so well there will never be another." His career as a bookmaker received no mention.

Lieutenant James "Curt" Riley was promoted to captain in early 1937 and went on to become chief of police before his retirement in 1949.

In August 1942, former chief of police and superintendent George A. Black died of a cerebral hemorrhage at his sister's home on Lovering Avenue. The news story of his death said, "Mr. Black resigned from the superintendency December 8, 1936 when the Board of Public Safety investigated the police bureau." No other mention was made of the corruption scandal.

The bawdy houses? Bill Frank claimed that the Edna Powell affair sparked a "cry for reform. That reform meant not only the phasing out of the city's established brothels, but also a major shake-up in the police department."

And the numbers business? "The [state] lottery wiped out the bookmakers," said retired cop Tom Monahan. "You can bet legally now."

# 2

# THREE GUN WILSON
# AND THE END OF PROHIBITION
# IN DELAWARE

## The Driest State in a Dry Nation

On September 24, 1930, Three Gun Wilson came to town. His arrival in Wilmington from Pittsburgh was feared by some and heralded by others, and within a few days, he was on the front page of all the local newspapers. Prohibition had its new champion in Delaware.

The Eighteenth Amendment to the U.S. Constitution, which outlawed the manufacture, sale and transportation of intoxicating liquors, was passed by the requisite number of states by January 1919 and went into effect on January 16, 1920. Delaware hadn't waited for national Prohibition to sweep the nation before taking its own action. By the 1897 State Constitution, Delaware had been divided into four local option districts—the city of Wilmington, the balance of New Castle County, Kent County and Sussex County. Kent and Sussex Counties voted against the license of liquor sales in 1907. At a special election in 1917, the New Castle County district that excluded Wilmington followed suit and voted itself "dry." Only Wilmington voted to stay "wet."

In 1919, the Delaware General Assembly decided to take the national Prohibition enforcement law, the Volstead Act, a few steps further with the passage in Delaware of the Klair Law. Named after a state representative from Mill Creek Hundred, Aaron F. Klair, this Delaware law, along with the so-called Loose Law passed in 1917, made it illegal to possess more than a

International Union of United Brewery Workers, Local 267, Wilmington, Delaware, circa 1910. Author's maternal grandfather, John Desmond, pictured in center of group, second row from top. *Courtesy of John Medkeff Jr.*

quart of alcohol and disallowed the medicinal use of alcohol. At least by the letter of the law, Delaware was the driest state in a dry nation.

By 1930, a decade of Prohibition had passed and lax enforcement plus a general disregard for the constitutional amendment and the various dry laws left Delaware afloat in illegal alcohol. Enforcement of state laws was left to the attorney general's office, who had little in the way of manpower. The state police (originally called the Delaware State Highway Police) was created in 1923 and was focused on mostly traffic issues. By 1930, the size of that force was forty-eight officers, charged with patrolling all of the state's highways. Local constables and police were limited in their capacity to enforce liquor laws and often were uninterested in such violations, particularly in Wilmington, which never wanted to be dry in the first place.

It was left to the federal government's Treasury Department to enforce Prohibition, and Delaware was assigned four officers to cover the entire state. It was no contest. From the traditional stills in rural Delaware to Whiskey Beach north of Rehoboth, where rumrunners brought their goods ashore, Delaware was much like the rest of America—alcohol could make its way into the glasses of anyone looking for a drink. Nowhere in Delaware, though, was Prohibition flouted as brazenly as in the city of Wilmington.

In 1920, Wilmington was by far the largest city in the state of Delaware, just as today. Wilmington's 110,000 citizens represented 74 percent of the total New Castle County population and 46 percent of the entire state's population, more than Kent and Sussex Counties combined. In addition to being home of the Du Pont Company, shipyards, leather tanneries and breweries made Wilmington a manufacturing hub. Three Wilmington breweries dominated the state's brewing industry prior to Prohibition, and their output made brewing the sixth-most valuable industry in Wilmington. The Hartman & Fehrenbach Brewery on Lovering Avenue and Scott Streets, the Diamond State Brewery at Fifth and Adams Streets and the Bavarian Brewery at Fifth and DuPont Streets, plus smaller brewers, bottlers

Daniel McElwee's Saloon, Fifth and Tatnall Streets, Wilmington, Delaware, circa 1890. *Collections of the Delaware Historical Society.*

and saloons, provided hundreds of jobs for the ethnic communities of Irish, Italian, German and Polish immigrants throughout the city. And the hub for these immigrant communities was often the neighborhood saloon.

This pattern held true across the nation, as urban areas were generally considered "wet" while the more rural sections of the country were "dry." As Daniel Okrent says in his book *Last Call: The Rise and Fall of Prohibition*, "Generally speaking, the more rural the state, the more arid the vote." But if "wet" Wilmington represented so great a portion of the state's population, how did Delaware ever pass Prohibition in the first place? In the years before the U.S. Supreme Court's ruling in 1962 to champion the premise of "One Man, One Vote" in *Baker v. Carr*, many states across the nation were dominated by the so-called rotten borough legislatures. Rural areas with small populations held disproportionate control over their states by being overrepresented in their number of state legislators. This was true in Delaware, as was pointed out in *Delaware: A History of the First State*: "Even after the adoption of the state constitution in 1897, which gave New Castle County a greater representation in the Senate and the House than either of the other two counties, Kent and Sussex by combining their power could still outvote the northern county in both branches of the legislature.

This was true in spite of the fact that…by 1900 the total number of people living in that city [Wilmington] was larger than the combined populations of the two lower counties."

To secure passage of the Eighteenth Amendment, Delaware governor John G. Townsend Jr. called for a special session of the general assembly on March 11, 1918. The combined vote in the House and Senate was overwhelmingly in favor of Prohibition, 40–9. This seeming dichotomy between voters and their legislatures was also evident in other states, where voters in Missouri and Ohio rejected dry amendments in statewide referendums, yet their legislatures voted for Prohibition by overwhelming majorities in the same year.

Delaware businesses did what they could to adapt to the new reality of Prohibition. The Joseph Stoeckle Brewing Company began producing near beer products, DublinXX and Golden Hop, and soft drinks. The Hartmann & Fehernbach Brewing Company changed its name to H&F Products Company and also began producing and distributing near beer and soda. The city's other brewery, the Bavarian Brewery, also converted production to soft drinks and cereal beverages as Peninsula Products Company. All of the former breweries failed in the early 1920s as the meager sales from nonalcoholic beverages could not sustain the expenses of hulking physical plants. According to Mike Kelly, a member of the Kelly family who have run the Logan House on Delaware Avenue in Wilmington for generations, the Logan House reverted to a hotel rather than selling illegal booze. The Delaware Bottling Company ran ads for Esslinger's Old Style Lager, "The Kick within the Law." Claiming "near beer" simply will not do, you could "drink it all evening at party or bridge—without a regret."

After ten years, though, Delawareans had had about enough of the Prohibition experiment. An editorial in the *Delmarva Star* stated, "By 1932 or before the compelling political issue in this country will be prohibition." The editorial promoted the idea of a referendum with the sole question: "Shall the Eighteenth Amendment be repealed?" As for its justification for such action, the paper said, "We believe the number who are sick and tired of the whole prohibition farce are overwhelmingly in the majority and they are entitled to be able to express their convictions in an election that has no other issues to complicate it. Let us have a referendum on Prohibition in Delaware."

## ENTER "THREE GUN" WILSON

Prohibition remained the law of the land, and Republican Herbert Hoover had been elected president in 1928 on a party platform supporting its enforcement. And if there was ever an incorruptible true believer in Prohibition, it was the deputy assigned to the Pittsburgh area in 1930, Harold G. "Three Gun" Wilson. Wilson was born in Kansas in 1884 and moved to Massachusetts before enlisting in the aviation corps during World War I. Wilson had served as a Prohibition official from the beginning, originally serving as chief prohibition enforcement officer in his home state of Massachusetts. On December 20, 1921, he received a report from one of his agents that "nearly all the Republican leaders of Massachusetts are down at a dinner [for] Governor Cox....It was a regular, old-time drinking carousal." Wilson assembled his agents and headed for the Quincy House Hotel, unafraid of the consequences of taking on the powerful Republican establishment. Once gaining admittance to the affair on the second floor of the hotel, the raiders confiscated large amounts of gin and whiskey, removing it to his headquarters.

Wilson was unaware of two facts when he conducted his raid that night. One, the event was to announce the candidacy of its guest of honor, Governor Channing H. Cox, for a second term as governor. Two, Wilson's superior, State Director of Prohibition Elmer C. Potter, was attending the banquet and had issued a waiver for the booze to be transported to the hotel. On January 27, 1922, Harold Wilson was removed as chief prohibition enforcement officer for Massachusetts by the United States commissioner of Internal Revenue. In a statement quoted in Wilson's book, *Dry Laws and Wet Politicians*, the federal prohibition commissioner conceded, "I [Wilson] was one of the best enforcement officials in the country, but added I was sometimes unduly energetic and too indiscreet." Reinstated when the Prohibition office was put under civil service protection, he served in several jurisdictions, including West Virginia and Pittsburgh, Pennsylvania. In Wheeling, West Virginia, he stated, "Conditions...were so rotten that even my agent in charge of that district...was under suspicion."

In Pittsburgh, Wilson continued his campaign against "wet" politicians with two very public raids. In May 1930, Wilson led thirty Prohibition agents armed with a search warrant on a raid of the Show Boat, a floating nightclub anchored in the Allegheny River. The boat was packed with three hundred people in the dining room and another one hundred in the gambling rooms, more than half of them in evening dress. The only liquor found was on the tables. Roulette wheels and dice tables were confiscated, and four arrests were made. The floating nightclub was padlocked for a year in June by order of a federal judge.

Wilson was placed in charge of the Pittsburgh District in July and quickly took on an even more sensitive political target, the Amen Corner Picnic. Described by the *Pittsburgh Press* as "one of the city's most famous social and semi-political organizations," the Amen Club was founded by a group of "congenial" politicians and businessmen that included thousands of Pittsburgh's best-known citizens. The agents first mingled with the four hundred men just arriving for the picnic and, on a command from Wilson, confiscated a number of barrels of "real beer." "Confusion Reigns as Crowd Rebels" headlined the press coverage as the picnickers jostled with the agents before the beer was hauled off.

Harold D. "Three Gun" Wilson, deputy Prohibition administrator for Delaware, 1930–32. Pittsburgh Press, *February 19, 1931, Courtesy of Delaware Historical Society.*

Rumors swirled that Wilson had finally gone too far, and by September, the national Prohibition director had transferred Wilson to Wilmington, Delaware. Wilson refused to go and was suspended for disobeying an order from his superiors. This prompted a meeting of Wilson, national Prohibition director Amos W.W. Woodcock and John D. Pennington, head of Prohibition enforcement for Pennsylvania, New Jersey and Delaware. Wilson finally relented and accepted his new post. His boss insisted there was no political pressure involved in the transfer and that the move was for the "good of the service." In his farewell speech quoted in the *Pittsburgh Gazette*, Wilson said, "I am a genuine dry and sincerely believe in the Cause. Now I am ordered to Delaware, a still further reduction. I am a soldier, however, enlisted in the Cause and will carry on, cheerfully, enthusiastically whether in Pittsburgh, Delaware or Honolulu."

Harold Wilson was by no means your typical Prohibition agent. He combined the two-fisted enforcement techniques of his Chicago counterpart, Elliott Ness, with the impassioned oratory of Prohibition-era evangelist Billy Sunday. As far as his colorful moniker "Three Gun," its origin has been variously ascribed to three guns he supposedly carried, or three guns he had mounted over his desk, or perhaps not to his arsenal of firearms at all but to his three-pronged "Wilson Method" approach to implementing Prohibition. In the preface of Wilson's book, *Dry Law Facts Not Fiction*, Reverend James W. Colona, pastor of the Harrison Street M.E. Church in Wilmington, wrote:

> *Mr. Wilson is a triple threat to all violators and nullifiers of the laws of State and Nation:*
>
> *First, Because he is an enforcement raider, energetic, daring and relentless. The bootleggers know from experience that he is apt to bring the law into their dens of iniquity at any time of night or day. The politicians know he is no respecter of persons. All violators look alike to him.*
>
> *Second, Because he is a speaker and writer who has the gift of saying and writing things that command attention....His everlastingly persistent and utterly fearless exposures of the lawlessness of the forces of evil are increasingly breaking up the iniquitous business of liquor law violation.*
>
> *Third, Because he is an organizer and a leader.*

With his history of self-promotion, the only thing that can be said with some certainty is that Harold Wilson indeed awarded the "Three Gun" title to himself.

The headlines in the *Wilmington Morning News* the day after Wilson's arrival announced, "Prohibition Heads Coming to Plan Drying Up State." The story stated, "Mr. Wilson made an extended and personal inspection of his district in preparation for the famous 'Wilson Method' which includes a strict enforcement of the Prohibition law, and educational campaign and close cooperation between city, state and federal officials." A meeting set up by Wilson and sponsored by the City Federation of the Woman's Christian Temperance Union (WCTU) was held at the newly constructed YMCA at Delaware Avenue and Washington Streets. More than one hundred citizens, including U.S. senator Daniel O. Hastings, were on hand to hear Wilson and national Prohibition director Colonel A.W.W. Woodcock discuss new plans to bring stricter liquor enforcement to Delaware.

Colonel Woodcock ignored his previous transfer confrontation with Harold Wilson and spoke in praise of him, saying, "We propose to have absolute enforcement of the Prohibition law in Delaware under Mr. Wilson's direction." Wilson himself said, "Let us enforce the Prohibition law where it is violated for commercial gain. Education and public sentiment will eventually take care of the drinkers. My only exception to this rule is such situations as when high public officials, sworn to uphold the laws of the

Cartoon by Hungerford, Pittsburgh Post Gazette, when I was transferred from Pittsburgh, Pa., to Wilmington, Del.

Cartoon from *Pittsburgh Post-Gazette* on Wilson's Transfer to Delaware. *From* Dry Law Facts Not Fiction *by Harold D. Wilson, courtesy of Hagley Museum and Library.*

nation and state, publicly flout the liquor and gambling laws. Then it is time to make example of them, regardless of whether their violation is for commercial gain or simply for stomach gratification."

Wilson had already begun his survey of his new Delaware territory and Wilmington, in particular. In a city that reportedly had 186 licensed saloons in 1917, 45 of these old-style "swinging door" saloons were still open for business after ten years of Prohibition, in addition to numerous speakeasies. At a follow-up meeting at the YMCA on October 15, 1930, a committee of ten men was selected to head up a Wilmington Citizens Survey to ascertain how many saloons and speakeasies operated in Wilmington and the conditions present in those establishments. According to Wilson, two hundred men from twenty different churches responded to the challenge to conduct the survey. This was a key part of the Wilson Method, to make the political leaders of a jurisdiction face up to actual conditions while at the same time educating the public. "You may oppose the principle of Prohibition and still be a 100% American citizen, but you cannot condone and encourage violation of law and be listed as such," stated Wilson. His proposed "Fact Finding and Law Supporting Committee" would not be a vigilante group, he assured listeners. "Deserving officials will be supported and drones and grafters should be eliminated from the service, whether Federal, State or County." Wilson was putting local officials on notice.

While his public persona was actively promoting education of the public, behind the scenes, he was putting together a strike force to bring enforcement to Wilmington. On October 25, Wilson struck. With his crew of four enforcement officers, Wilson raided fifteen establishments across Wilmington, one of which would haunt the rest of his time in Delaware. In ten barrooms, Wilson's crew found old-time bars and fixtures but no patrons, bringing into question how much surprise was really a factor. However, in the other six establishments, he found anywhere from a handful of men drinking and a few pints of liquor to more substantial operations crowded with drinkers. At the Labor Lyceum at 412 DuPont Street, Wilson and his raiders found two barrels of beer, while at 108 West Seventh there were thirty men bellying up to the bar as the proprietor, Malcolm McCoy, tried to destroy the evidence. According to McCoy and his attorney, Wilson entered the cigar store and passed through swinging doors to the bar area without a search warrant. After Wilson grabbed McCoy, McCoy pulled away and broke a liquor bottle over a step to destroy the evidence. Wilson came up behind him and struck him on the head with his blackjack, saying, "You will get rough with Three-Gun Wilson, will you?" Wilson insisted that he acted in self-defense and that the blow he gave McCoy was a "love tap."

The highlight of the nighttime raid was, as the *Wilmington Morning News* characterized it on the front page, "Democratic Club Raided by Wilson, Yields No Liquor":

> *An evening of raiding activities on the part of Harold D. "Three-Gun" Wilson and four federal Prohibition agents Saturday was climaxed with their descent shortly before midnight on the headquarters of the Democratic League, 610 French Street, which adjoins the headquarters of the Democratic City Committee, where Wilson alleged an old-fashioned, horseshoe bar was doing a thriving business....*
>
> *No sooner had he [Wilson] and his men stepped into the quarters than they were recognized and jeered by a score of men, in the building, who impeded their work.*

*Before the agents could begin seizing evidence, two bartenders are alleged to have scooped up glasses containing alleged liquor and smashed them and making their escape through some panels in the rear of the bar. Mr. Wilson also alleged that shortly after he entered the building, an unidentified person ran back of the structure, knocking the bungs out of several barrels of beer and destroying this evidence.*

The interference was more than breaking some glasses or pouring out beer. Two agents were "struck and shoved about" when they tried to gather evidence. In the end, no liquor was confiscated at the Democratic League, but Wilson took down the names of the patrons, with the threat of having them arrested on charges of assault and battery and interfering with the work of an officer, "if the agents can identify the men." Included in this group were the former city Democratic chairman and a former city councilman.

The next night at a speech at the Harrison Street M.E. Church, Wilson elaborated on his method of taking names. "Many questions have been asked as to why I took the names and addresses of the drinking temperance advocates of the Democratic League. I shall recommend to the United States District Attorney that all be subpoenaed for federal grand jury and given an opportunity to tell, under oath, what they know of the Democratic Club nuisance. And unfortunately for them I have plenty of evidence to make truthful statements quite advisable. This is a course that I hope to follow with the so-called better class drinkers."

As for the other members of the establishment:

*It is nonsense to maintain that the members of the Democratic League did not know what was going on in their club. Such a big completely stocked and well-patronized bar must have been known to the members. It was the largest and best equipped barroom I have seen in Delaware, liquor was very plentiful and every precaution had been taken to guard it against the law. The barroom was so well protected that it was even locked against the casual visitor who might have gained entrance to the lobby to the club through two locked doors. This liquor joint was maintained as a sort of sanctum-sanctorum, sacred unto those who had demonstrated their prowess with the god of Bacchus.*

Already, questions were arising about the legality of Wilson's tactics. He had somehow obtained a passkey to the Democratic League, which got him through three sets of locked doors before he came to the bar. As was his practice, Wilson chose not to obtain a warrant before conducting the raid. He said in a later speech,

> *I have been asked times innumerable why I did not get a Federal Search Warrant for the Democratic League raid. The answer is three-fold:*
>
> *First: No Federal Warrant can issue without a signed affidavit and this affidavit must be made out by someone who has actually seen the violation, and the affidavit is a matter of public record. Consequently, the members who gave me information would have been exposed.*
>
> *Second: It is practically impossible to get a Federal Warrant for service during the night-time without a buy.*
>
> *Third: My men and I went to the Club to buy liquor. An open violation is always preferable to a raid with a Search Warrant, because of the endless legal technicalities surrounding a warrant. Consequently, I never use a warrant when I can possibly get along without it.*

Regardless of their legality, Wilson pressed on with more raids in Wilmington two weeks later. This time, he changed tactics and personnel, taking advantage of the groundwork laid by undercover agents. Wilson described the raids in his book:

> *On November 7 and 8 I directed a series of raids on 18 barrooms in the City of Wilmington. Ten agents were borrowed from the Philadelphia office permitting the raiding of 6 of these places simultaneously at the zero hour of 4 PM on Friday November 7. After locking up our prisoners my agents apparently went home and the Philadelphia contingent headed for the Quaker City. The men, however, had orders to meet at a rendezvous some 4 miles outside the city at 9 PM, where plans were laid for another sortie into the city. The bootleggers were caught napping and 5 more places knocked off. The next day in order to catch them off guard again, the zero hour was set at noon and seven more places raided. One of the greatest essentials to successful raiding is hitting at unexpected times. My first raids in Wilmington were all staged on Saturdays. This big series of raids was started on Friday as the bootleggers expected operations on a Saturday. In the history of Wilmington two consecutive raids had not occurred the same day so the surprise attack on Friday worked beautifully. No noon raids had previously been staged, consequently the bootleggers were again caught napping.*

Newspaper accounts of the raids presented a much less "beautiful" version of events. The November 8 *Morning News* story "Riot Call Sent to Aid Wilson in Liquor Raids" claimed several agents had narrow escapes from serious injury by friends of those arrested. The newspaper reported, "At Seventh and Lincoln Streets, it was necessary to send a squad of four policemen to protect the raiders and their prisoners. The automobile in which the agents traveled was badly damaged, the tires being slashed, and sand thrown in the motor….Another outbreak of spectators occurred when the agents entered 6 W. Seventh Street….An onlooker was said to have been struck by a milk bottle which was apparently aimed at the government agents." The newspaper also noted "An innovation as far as local dry operations are concerned, was the taking of flashlight pictures in all places visited. Wilson said these photos would be used to show the character of the places entered."

Not all the raids were taking place in so-called "dens if iniquity." *Wilmington Morning News* columnist Bill Frank recounted a tale of illegal liquor sales going on in the center of Wilmington respectability, the Hotel du Pont. "A well-known Wilmington bootlegger delivered whiskey to The Hotel in dress boxes and men's clothing boxes, marked with emblems of prominent Wilmington stores," according to Frank. "This ploy worked pretty well for some time until an alert bellman decided that a lot of clothing was being purchased by hotel guests. The then federal Prohibition agent, 'Three Gun' Wilson registered himself as a guest at The Hotel and observed what was going on. He discovered that a group of bootleggers had rented six rooms on the second floor and were carrying on their business. It appeared that the liquor was being received from a boat off Delaware City.

"Within four days after he registered as a guest, Wilson pulled off a spectacular Hotel du Pont raid, and that ended that."

Wilson's tactics were having their desired effects. By mid-November, he had federal court orders to padlock thirteen saloons as nuisance properties. "In some quarters I have been termed the most unpopular man in the state," Wilson proclaimed. "I glory in this unpopularity." He also was very willing to burnish his tough guy image. As he relates in his book, "On one of the raids in Wilmington, Delaware, one of the hangers-on started to get obstreperous, another bum took him aside and whispered in a clearly audible voice, 'Sh, sh, that's Three Gun—he has been on a thousand raids and will blow your brains out and say nothing.'"

In a speech after the raids, Wilson discussed the character of the bootleggers he targeted: "One of the amusing features of all the raids and in fact one of the most helpful sources of information is the always present

Photo by Rumer, Newark, Del.

Destroying a Miscellaneous Seizure of Stills, Coils, Steam Boilers, Etc.

Harold D. Wilson destroying stills in Delaware *From* Dry Law Facts Not Fiction *by Harold D. Wilson, courtesy of Hagley Museum and Library.*

suspicion and jealousy of bootleggers regarding each other. They are all crooks and they know it, and when one bootlegger can get another put out of business he feels competition will be just so much less keen, consequently we are always getting information from them."

Addressing the growing controversy about the Democratic League raid two weeks previous, Wilson teased, "I might suggest to the members of the Democratic Club, who are making such wild endeavors to find out who supplied me with a key and a chart to the holy of holies within the club, that they check up on some of the bootlegger members of their organization. A little checking along this line might reveal the source of my information and eliminate a lot of worrying."

On one point, though, Wilson was clearly not teasing. As the results of Wilson's two hundred Citizens Survey, regarding saloons and speakeasies in Wilmington, came in, he was damning. The survey revealed forty-one saloons and seventy-four speakeasies were operating in the city of Wilmington, focused on the downtown area, Union Street and "the Polish section of Browntown." In some instances, the saloons and speakeasies had the apparent backing of police officers. "At one place between 800 and 900 Madison St. the checkers had considerable difficulty getting by the policeman who was apparently guarding the dive," stated Wilson. "In another case between 700 and 800 Shipley St., two officers in uniform were noted trying to enter a well-known dive. The place was locked. These policemen then went down the street where they met the proprietor, a well-known bootlegger, and with him went back to the dive. The officers soon came out wiping their mouths." As he would say in his book, "Some of the citizens who engaged in the Wilmington, Delaware liquor survey in October and November 1930 can testify as to the proficiency of some of the Wilmington police in guarding the speakeasies against strangers." Wilson concluded, "Practically every one of these dives could be closed in 30 days if a sincere and determined effort was made to do so. There is not a liquor dive, gambling den or bawdy house that is doing business of any size in this city the police do not know the location and its habitués."

With this, Wilson had expanded his target list from bootleggers and their patrons to political leaders in the city and now to the Wilmington administration and its police department. Within weeks, the directors of the Public Safety Commission for Wilmington were asking for the resignation of George Black, superintendent of Public Safety. Black, who had been chief of police and then superintendent since 1902, was informed by Dr. Washburn, president of the Public Safety Board, that a younger man was desired for the position. As was reported by the *Wilmington Morning News*, "Every effort was made on the part of the directors to keep the matter quiet. It was hinted that the recent wholesale raid on alleged barrooms and speakeasies about the city by Deputy Prohibition [*sic*] Harold D. Wilson caused the directors to believe it was a reflection on the police department and caused the action."

The issue came to a head at the November 25, 1930 meeting of the board. In a prepared statement, President Washburn said, "The Superintendent of the Department of Public Safety has been asked to retire because in the mature considerate judgment of the Directors the best interests of the Department and of the City demand a re-organization. It has been apparent to the directors that the increasing scope of police activities involving as they do problems of liquor law enforcement, traffic control, the development of new methods of training with which to cope with the modern criminal has been beyond the capacity of the Superintendent." Black, however, would not go quietly. "With his face flushed after hearing the charges read," said the *Morning News*, "Superintendent Black shouted a strong defiance to the board that 'I will not resign.'"

In spite of the charges, Black seemed to have the support of many community members, including several pastors of local churches. The two other directors sided with Black in the end, and President Washburn's motion to relieve Superintendent Black was defeated. The Reverend Francis Tucker, pastor of St. Anthony's Roman Catholic Church, was reported to be among the first to congratulate Black for refusing to resign. Tucker was an outspoken opponent of Prohibition and was quoted on the subject by the *Delmarva Star* upon his return from Rome, Italy, the following January, stating, "Prohibition still makes us the laughingstock of the world. They laugh at its hypocrisy in the face of the 98% of the American violators who drink abroad openly and, safe to imagine, at home when they can. And they laugh at the inferiority complex it creates in an otherwise superior people, who are made to believe by its doctrine that they cannot hold its liquor like Europeans."

Wilson was not about to let up on the local public officials, though. In a speech at the Second Baptist Church in December, he said, "Where do our public officials stand on the recent attempt to close and padlock some of Wilmington's most disreputable saloons? I have heard nothing from them and I doubt whether the U.S. District Attorney, Mr. Wales, or our U.S. Judge, John P. Nields, has heard one word of encouragement."

# A DIFFERENT KIND OF OPPONENT

Three Gun Wilson was accustomed to fighting with bootleggers and wet politicians, even police forces indifferent at best if not corrupted by the forces of evil as he saw it. "It is time we started using expressive verbiage in branding the cheap, skulking good for nothing, liquor crazed proprietors and denizens of the booze hellholes....They care not how many women and children suffer because his satanic majesty's first assistant, the liquor dispenser, gets the money that should go for food and shoes for the children." This was his battlefield, promoting "Christian Citizenship" as a way to defeat opponents of Prohibition. He did not believe the dry laws were as unenforceable as some claimed: "It can be enforced, it is being enforced much better than generally admitted and will be enforced with ample effectiveness when the great American public actually wakes up to the absurdity of allowing a few power and money crazed politicians to manhandle a great, easily prejudiced, foreign minded, city population to the detriment of the rest of the nation."

Wilson was not shy about identifying his opponents as the recent immigrants congregating in the country's metropolitan areas. He was also not above using ethnic slurs when claiming he knew firsthand "the type of men who are bootlegging, greasy, low-down, good-for-nothing parasites, too lazy and too crooked to even attempt to make an honest living."

Wilson had another opponent, though, who didn't fit his caricature of the greasy, foreign-minded city population or those too lazy to make an honest living. In room 4150 of the Du Pont Building in downtown Wilmington, a few blocks from the new YMCA that hosted many of Wilson's talks, was the headquarters of the Delaware division of the Association Against the Prohibition Amendment (AAPA). This organization had been around since before the passage of the Eighteenth Amendment but had taken on new significance and influence when a new chairman took over in 1927. That year, one of the nation's richest men, a powerful industrialist and arguably the most dominant figure in Delaware, Pierre S. du Pont, became chairman of the national group and a leading voice for Prohibition's repeal.

Since its inception, this organization had attracted the membership of America's East Coast blue bloods, like Stuyvesant Fish, Kermit Roosevelt, Marshall Field and Vincent Astor. Daniel Okrent states, though, "The AAPA failed to establish meaningful traction until it won the attention, in 1926, of Pierre S. du Pont—chairman of the family's chemical colossus; chairman of the du Pont—controlled General Motors Corporation; and soon the dominant figure in an invigorated AAPA."

Three Gun Wilson's work clearly followed his passion, but it was less clear why Pierre S. du Pont would want to get involved in such an issue. The "wets," as portrayed by many dry proponents, were the beer- and wine-swilling ethnic people populating the big cities who sought to overrule the majority of right-thinking Americans in favor of strict Prohibition. The AAPA, on the other hand, took a far different view of Prohibition. It was founded in 1918 by conservative attorney William H. Slayton, who told his friend H.L. Mencken that he viewed the law as overly intrusive Progressive Era legislation. What's more, Slayton was "particularly alarmed" not only by Prohibition but also by a proposed amendment abolishing child labor, which he said meant "the management of the family would be taken out of the control of parents." Slayton successfully recruited du Pont's righthand man, John Raskob, to his organization, but Pierre du Pont initially resisted. According to Dr. Ranjit S. Dighe, Prohibition was suspect to du Pont "both because it expanded government's reach into people's private activities and because it was unenforceable. Pierre further assailed Prohibition as 'the worst kind of tyranny' of the majority and said it opened the door for 'further curtailment of our liberties if a majority can be brought to bear on any subject.'"

But it was another proposed Delaware law, the Weer bill, which would have banned the possession of any liquor at all, that spurred Pierre du Pont and his brothers Irenee and Lammot into action. Pierre spoke out against the Weer bill, and in 1925, it was defeated in Delaware's general assembly. With his brothers already members of AAPA along with his trusted advisor John Raskob, Pierre du Pont joined up with the repeal movement by 1927. Another motivating factor for du Pont's change of heart was one that struck far closer to home. True, in Pierre du Pont's view, the Eighteenth Amendment and its following laws curtailed liberties, involved government in peoples' private lives and was unenforceable, but its very existence was presaged and enabled by a far more insidious amendment, the Sixteenth.

Up until the time of the passage of the Sixteenth, or income tax, Amendment the primary source of income for the federal government was liquor taxes. "By 1875 onward," said Daniel Okrent, "fully one-quarter of federal revenues came from the beer keg and the whiskey bottle, a proportion that in 1913 would lead a prominent temperance leader to describe this generous source of funds, not inaccurately, as 'a bribe on the public conscience.'" Okrent further wrote that "by 1910 the federal government was drawing more than $200 million a year from the bottle and the keg—71 percent of all internal revenue, and more than 30 percent of federal revenue overall."

The federal government clearly couldn't do without this amount of revenue and survive, but the Sixteenth Amendment changed all of that. As profits for the Du Pont Company soared with the beginning of World War I in 1914, so did taxes on the family that controlled it. President Wilson funded the buildup of American forces through the Revenue Act of 1916, which doubled income tax rates on the highest brackets, created the first peacetime inheritance tax and assessed a 12.5 percent levy on munitions manufacturers. An exceptionally wealthy man who, by some accounts, earned more and paid more taxes than any other American in 1929, Pierre du Pont was singularly assaulted by the switch from liquor-based to income-based taxation. He was also a singularly talented and effective administrator accustomed to getting his way. His takeover of the AAPA meant he intended to overturn the offending Prohibition Amendment.

Pierre du Pont remade the AAPA organization first, transforming its leadership by imitating the Du Pont Company's board of directors and executive committee format, with himself and his brothers in top positions. Then he remade the group's arguments against Prohibition to mirror his own thoughts. Through pamphlets, radio addresses, magazine articles and political donations, the AAPA inserted itself into the nation's debate about the Eighteenth Amendment. In a 1929 radio talk titled "A Business Man's View of Prohibition," du Pont said that "people flout the law, causing national scandal." He also declared the law fundamentally invalid because it lacked the consent of the governed.

But du Pont had more on his mind than just the lawlessness caused by the Eighteenth Amendment. As he said in a letter to a friend in 1928, "The object of the Association [AAPA] is not merely the return of the use of alcoholic beverages in the United States. Another important factor is the tremendous loss of revenue to our Government through the Prohibition laws." With repeal, du Pont told his friend, "the revenue of our government would be increased sufficiently to warrant the abolition of the income tax and corporate tax."

According to a paper sponsored by the National Commission on Marijuana and Drug Abuse titled "History of Alcohol Prohibition," by January 1931, the AAPA had almost $3 million to put toward the election of "wet" congressmen. Regarding the source of the funds, AAPA depended on a number of converts from the dry cause. "In 1928 the du Pont family abandoned the drys, followed…by John D. Rockefeller and S.S. Kresge. Their conversion was effected under the strong influence of the income tax. Doggedly, Pierre S. du Pont circulated a brochure concluding that 'the British liquor policy applied in the United States would permit the total abolition of the income tax both personal and corporate.'"

A pamphlet called *Food for Thought*, published by the Delaware AAPA, lists those who have been made criminals by this law, including "every doctor in Delaware who has administered brandy, whisky…to a sick person, even though he believed such stimulant was necessary to save the patient's life." As for results of Prohibition, it lists first that "it has deprived the individual of that personal liberty which all men cherish and have fought and died for." It goes on to list sixteen devastating effects of Prohibition on American society, from filling the federal courts with low-level criminal cases to drawing millions of dollars from taxpayers in a futile effort to suppress the liquor traffic and ending with, "The church has lost much of its power for good in the community because it has now gotten into politics and is devoting its energy to political rather than religious questions." The pamphlet drew on religious, ideological and practical arguments against

Photo by Rumer, Newark, Del.

The Old Swinging Doors That Swing No More

A padlocked saloon in Wilmington, Delaware, thanks to Three Gun Wilson. *From* Dry Law Facts Not Fiction *by Harold D. Wilson, courtesy of Hagley Museum and Library.*

Prohibition, trying to appeal to the broadest audience possible. This was Pierre du Pont's approach.

Such high-level opposition did nothing to discourage Three Gun Wilson from his campaign to rid Delaware of alcohol. Raids in Wilmington continued arising from undercover buys of liquor made by agents on loan from the New Jersey district, and cases requesting locations be padlocked were coming before the federal commissioner. Wilson's public pressure on Wilmington officials seemed to have had an effect, as more raids by the city's vice squad received press coverage. Wilson remained the face of enforcement and the focus of those opposed to Prohibition. Some opposition came in the form of threats on his life. One particular threat, in a letter released to the press in November 1930, was very specific: "I want to give you a little bit of warning. You stay away from Lincoln Street, or you will need more than 3 guns. I think the best thing for you to do is leave this town and stay away if you value your life. You think you are doing something great. But you are making a damn fool of yourself. You are making the State worse than it was before. Because there are going to be a killing and you will be the stiff. Stay away from Little Italy."

Wilson made light of the threats and wrote about his rumored death later. "My death from shooting was quite generally broadcast throughout the city and State one Saturday afternoon," Wilson wrote. "I left the office for down State about noon and as no one could get in touch with me for several hours my office was in a terrible state of agitation. The secretary and some of the agents wildly calling the hospitals and any other possible hibernating place for a corpse or potential corpse. Much to the relief of the force, I called in some two hours later to see if all was well and found much to my surprise that I was supposed to be dead."

## The Democratic League Hearing

As Three Gun Wilson's cases made their way before federal commissioners and judges, his methods came under fire from his targets, their attorneys and crowds attending the public hearings. Wilson did not hesitate in firing back: "For the past week my men and I have been subject to the scrutiny and sometimes the jeers of fifty or more bootleggers and their pals who have congregated each day at the hearings before the U.S. Commissioner. There may have been naturalized citizens and friends of the United States Government in these crowds, but I noted very few who could measure up to any real standard of American citizenship." In this address before the Sunday evening service in the Scott M.E. Church on November 16, 1930, Wilson was even more scathing toward the lawyers who represented the bootleggers. In answer to his own question about why so few criminals are convicted in our courts, Wilson answered,

> The answer to these questions, friends, is that we have so much red tape and so many legal technicalities in our court procedure, that fee worshipping lawyers can actually make a farce, in many instances, out of our courts of justice.... Time and again I have seen the very provisions of constitutional law designed to protect society perverted to protect the crook.
>
> Friends, I am not attacking the integrity of our courts or the great majority of our lawyers. Both in most instances are above reproach, but

*I am attacking the ethics of a profession which will permit a very small minority, probably not one-half of one percent, to feed as vultures on the ill-gotten funds of such "public enemies" as Al Capone and his gangsters.*

Further, he proclaimed, "Every man is entitled to his day in court, but the great law-respecting American public is entitled to protection against the alibi artists, the technicality magicians and the witness-intimidating attorneys who place their fee above the general welfare of humanity."

Why was Wilson so enraged by the legal profession? Several of his cases were being challenged in court by attorneys representing the targets of his raids, but this was to be expected anywhere. More distressing to Wilson was the dismissal of charges against some alleged bootleggers on technical issues, including out-of-date warrants used in his raids. A larger fight was looming, though, and it involved Wilson's highest profile case.

U.S. district attorney Leonard Wales announced at the end of December that the case of the Democratic League raid was to be heard in January 1931. Although no liquor was confiscated in the raid and no one was arrested, the Democratic League and its president, Adolph G. Dangel, were being charged with possession of alcohol over the legal limit and maintenance of a nuisance property. Dangel was an immigrant from Stuttgart, Germany, and would soon become the tax collector for the southern district of the city of Wilmington.

*Adolph & Dangel*

Adolph Dangel, president of the Democratic League of Delaware and Diamond State Brewery Inc. *From* Delaware, A History of the First State, *personal and family records.*

In January 1931, a petition involving the case of the *U.S. of A. v. Democratic League of Delaware* was heard before federal judge John P. Nields. Wilmington attorney John Biggs Jr. represented the defendant, the Democratic League of Delaware. Harold Wilson gave his testimony about what he and his agents found on the premises of the Democratic League and admitted to entering through the three locked doors to access the basement grill room and its horseshoe bar. Biggs seized on Wilson's admission and pointed out that he and his agents entered the premises without a search warrant. Did Wilson get information about law-breaking, a diagram of the premises and a key from a member, or was it stolen? In his petition, Biggs charged that due to a lack of a warrant, the federal agents were trespassers on the property and therefore had no grounds for the raid.

This is just what Wilson complained about in his church speeches, the "technicality magicians" who would divert the court's attention from violations of the Prohibition laws. The crux of Biggs's argument was that the league had constitutional protections against unwarranted searches, and the court seemed receptive. "Whether or not Mr. Wilson and his agents were justifiably and legally upon the premises of the Democratic League is certainly something which is pertinent to this petition," stated Biggs, "and to decide the pertinence of this petition we must know who that informant was, so as to test whether or not he was a member." It followed that if the league had constitutional protections, access could be granted only by someone with legal authority to do so. But did the league have such protections?

Judge Nields put that question to rest with the following ruling: "I think a Club is a house within the meaning of the 4th Amendment of the Constitution of the United States. That amendment secures a corporation as well as other people from an unreasonable search." Prosecuting attorney Leonard Wales complained, "There is no evidence here that it was used as a dwelling house and it had no immunity from search without a warrant." Judge Nields was having none of that argument, nor that the identity of the informant was privileged. Judge Nields stated, "I rule it is not a privileged communication and I overrule the objection and I direct the witness [Wilson] to answer."

Three Gun Wilson's most publicized raid had come down to this. For the case against the Democratic League to continue, Wilson had to reveal how he had obtained the key to the club. Wilson responded, "Your Honor, I will have to tell you that that was given to me in confidence and I cannot with honor disclose it." Judge Nields now delivered the ultimate indignity on the man sworn to uphold the law. "The Court adjudges you in contempt," intoned Nields, "and you are committed to the custody of the U.S. Marshal for this District, until you purge yourself of that contempt." As the *Evening Journal* put it, "The stormy petrel of the Prohibition service was then turned over to the marshal." Wilson came to court seeking to put a padlock on the Democratic League and found instead he was being led away in handcuffs.

The indignity of the contempt charge did not involve any real jail time, though, as U.S. marshal Charles P. Hanratty, in a show of professional courtesy, took Wilson instead to a hotel in his hometown of Smyrna, where Wilson spent the night. The next day, Wilson and his government attorneys filed an appeal of the contempt ruling to be held before the U.S. District

Court of Appeals, and Wilson was released on $1,000 bail. After the hearing, Wilson claimed that the person who gave him the key had approached him and said he was willing to reveal his name. "I am pleased to state that this person has offered to admit his identity and testify before the court. This proves that he has the nerve to come out in the open, but I asked him in view of the principle at stake not to disclose his identity."

While Wilson was battling for his freedom in federal court, Pierre S. du Pont was renewing his battle against Prohibition in the Delaware General Assembly, specifically for the right of Wilmingtonians to sell liquor. Given the privilege of the floor before a joint session of the general assembly on February 6, 1931, du Pont presented a petition signed by 39,700 Delaware residents to repeal the Klair Law. The petition was the result of du Pont's anti-Prohibition group sending letters to 106,000 citizens with a questionnaire on the repeal or retention of the Klair Law. The 44,500 responses received were overwhelmingly in favor of repeal—39,700 in favor and only 3,823 against.

"The Constitution of Delaware requires the General Assembly to offer a vote on 'Local Option' to a county or the city of Wilmington on the request of a majority of the Senators and Representatives elected from any one of these divisions," stated du Pont. He continued:

> *In 1917 the people of the city of Wilmington voted to continue the system of licensed sale. Notwithstanding this decision affecting half the population of the State, the General Assembly of 1919 violated the 'Local Option' rights retained by the people under their Constitution, and ratified the Eighteenth Amendment.*
>
> *The above laws* [referencing the Loose Law and Klair Law], *together with those of the United States, if enforced, would prevent absolutely the use of intoxicating liquor as a beverage. It appears, however, after several years' trial, that enforcement is not effective. Many citizens, even those of irreproachable character, do not hesitate to obtain and possess liquor for personal use and especially for medical purposes in violation of the law.*

DuPont's approach here, as in 1929, was not to overturn the Eighteenth Amendment but, in his words, "to make the laws of Delaware accord with the 18th Amendment…and, as far as possible, to the right of 'Local Option' retained by the people of Delaware." Later, he said, "The Klair Law, as far as it follows the Federal Constitution, is within the powers of the General Assembly but beyond this, dealing with medicinal liquor not prohibited by the Federal Constitution, the choice of the people of Wilmington especially and of the counties also, where sales of medicinal liquor was not prohibited by local option, the Constitution of the State should be respected." Du Pont could not win his ultimate prize in the Delaware General Assembly, but he could undermine the local laws and further weaken the entire Prohibition structure. Not to be outdone by the likes of the WCTU, du Pont employed his wife, Alice, to speak publicly from the women's point of view. At a meeting of the Women's Organization for National Prohibition Reform (WONPR), Mrs. du Pont stated that she was once in favor of the dry amendment but now claimed Prohibition was not a policy but a predicament and should be repealed.

While du Pont spoke of people of "irreproachable character" violating the Prohibition laws, Harold Wilson had a distinctly different take on these citizens. Just the day before du Pont's address to the general assembly, Wilson spoke to his Fact Finding and Law Supporting Committee for Wilmington at the YMCA, saying, "It has been my experience that I have found liquor, gambling, prostitution, obscene pictures and general filthy degeneration running hand in hand.

"I do not intend to infer by this statement that all who drink and gamble are depraved," Wilson continued, "but I do mean that the bootleggers, the professional gamblers and the white slavers are all of the same breed, and the so-called otherwise 'good citizen,' who patronizes any of these enemies of society, is inviting disaster for himself as well as his Government." As usual, Wilson was taking no prisoners in his verbal assaults on violators of the Eighteenth Amendment and had no qualms about opposing Delaware's most powerful and influential figure. He would go on to criticize du Pont's associate John Raskob, then head of the Democratic National Committee, who put forward a plan to modify the Eighteenth Amendment to allow states to manufacture and sell liquor. "This suggestion hardly warrants an answer," stated Wilson dismissively, "as it contains the double boomerang of putting State Governments into business and going backward to State Prohibition, which has been tried and found wanting."

Any proposal to weaken absolute prohibition was anathema to the abstentious Wilson. "I have yet to see a proposed form of liquor control that is not infinitely more complex and regulatory than the absolute prohibition of intoxicating liquors," Wilson said. "The Pierre S. du Pont Plan, the Anderson Plan and the Canadian System are all paternalistic. The amount of liquor, the place and time of purchase, an investigation of the personal habits of the would-be consumers are all provided for in the minutest detail."

Pierre S. du Pont also drew the ire of the Reverend C.T. Watson at the Methodist Episcopalian Conference that spring, specifically regarding the veracity of du Pont's poll on Prohibition. "Every man in Delaware has either received a favor from du Pont or is expecting one in a few weeks," said Reverend Watson. "I am a native-born Delawarean and I know....Of course, all who wanted to please Mr. du Pont made out their ballot wet and signed their name to it and sent it to his office. Those who could not conscientiously vote wet, hid their ticket in their family Bible or elsewhere, and did not vote at all."

## PROBLEMS WITH THE NOBLE EXPERIMENT

Raids on speakeasies and bootlegger joints continued throughout 1931, with the Wilmington vice squad handling most activity in Wilmington and Wilson raiding up and down the state. Wilson's forays into Sussex County yielded arrests in Seaford, Delmar and Lewes in February, while Wilson also organized another of his Fact-Finding and Law Supporting Committees in Delmar. The Wilmington vice squad found beer on tap at Eleventh and Jackson in May, a cache of several hundred bottles and 4 crocks of home brew on Lancaster Avenue in July and 140 bottles of home brew confiscated in September.

Wilson's contempt hearing in the U.S. Court of Appeals was filed in May and was scheduled to be heard later in the year. By the time it was heard in late November, U.S. district attorney Leonard Wales argued on Wilson's behalf to overturn the contempt charge, while a special assistant to the U.S. district attorney appointed specifically for this case opposed the motion to overturn. The various federal authorities, from Prohibition bureau agents to district attorneys to judges, were so intent on arguing with each other that the alleged violator of the Prohibition law became a bystander.

Wilson would continue his fast-paced raids or, as he called them, his "weekly inspection" into the fall, with ten to fifteen stops a night as the norm. Small quantities of booze would be destroyed at a few of the locations, but it was questionable how much impact these raids were having on all the illegal activity. Two raids in north Wilmington that fall highlighted Wilson's ongoing problems with Prohibition enforcement in Delaware. In October, the Embassy Night Club at Philadelphia Pike and Harvey Road was raided at the end of a swing of fifteen suspected speakeasies in Wilmington. The club had been under investigation for a few weeks, and Wilson and his agents obtained a search warrant for the place. When they entered and took seats at tables among the several score of diners and dancers, "the general atmosphere of the place indicated to the agents that the place had been 'tipped off' it was to be raided. Employees…were not surprised when the agents flashed a search warrant…and did not interfere with a search." No beer or empty beer barrels were found on the premises and the two quarts of liquor confiscated were all that remained from the two dozen discarded bottles. No arrests were made.

In November, the Gigolo Inn on Marsh Road near Arden was raided, again at the tail end of a string of raids of eleven other speakeasies. The Gigolo Inn had been a farmhouse until a few months before, when Perry's Tavern on Concord Pike had been shut down for violations of the Prohibition laws. The proprietor, Anthony Cotillo, had followed court instructions to dismantle the bar fixtures at the Perry Tavern but then moved them to the Marsh Road farmhouse, remodeled it and opened it as the Gigolo Inn. On the night of the raid, other agents had made liquor purchases before Wilson entered and made the arrest on Cotillo. A loaded shotgun and revolver were discovered behind the bar.

The consuming public, as demonstrated by the "scores of diners and dancers" at the Embassy Inn, had little or no regard for being raided by federal agents. It was almost a badge of honor to be part of the crowd that flouted the laws. And as was the case with the Gigolo Inn, there was no shortage of proprietors willing to go to great lengths to provide the means to violate the laws. After a dozen years of Prohibition, it was no wonder the general public was fed up with the so-called noble experiment.

In 1931, the federally appointed Wickersham Commission concluded that the country had prohibition in law but not in fact. According to the commission, "There was a general prevalence of drinking in homes, clubs and hotels.…Throughout the country people of wealth, businessmen and professional men and their families, and the higher paid workingmen and their families, are drinking in large numbers in open flouting of the law. And neither Congress nor the states set up adequate machinery or appropriated sufficient funds for the enforcement of the prohibitory legislation. Federal and state legislation, as a matter of fact, strove to satisfy so that, as was aptly said, the drys had their prohibition law and the wets had their liquor."

In December 1931, the Delaware WONPR, of which Alice du Pont was secretary, held a public meeting at Wilmington's New Century Club. The speaker, Ms. Jeanette Eckman, declared, "We have in the Prohibition reform organization today many women who were originally Prohibitionists, some of whom came slowly and reluctantly to the conclusion that Prohibition as a method has brought too many glaring evils in its train to be any longer useful in the cause of temperance. No one wants the saloon." The organization was willing to back the continuation of the local option in Delaware's constitution so that counties could decide their own situation.

Ms. Eckman went further than just criticizing Prohibition itself. She also targeted Three Gun Wilson and his enforcement tactics. "There is a serious side to the fanatical effort to enforce Prohibition in this State, which is being generally overlooked. The constitutional rights of the individual citizen are being violated without protest that should come from an alert citizenship." She continued:

> *If there is one right that has been regarded as inalienable, it is the right of the individual to be secure in his possessions and in his house from unreasonable search and seizure....Yet in Delaware it is not so maintained....You have probably read recently the statement of the local Federal enforcement agent that he prefers to get direct evidence of possession and sale by purchase rather than depend on a warrant—so jealous are the Federal Courts in which his cases must be tried, of the rights of the citizen, that the least thing wrong with the warrant throws out the evidence. How different in our Delaware court where a policeman may smash up property in an illegal search and if he finds anything still have the evidence used against the possessor....The illegal enforcement, even of just laws, does more to undermine justice than a harsh law in itself.*

For committed drys, having language such as that thrown back at them by the Delaware WONPR was turning the world on its head. To have their cause tarred with such phrases as "glaring evils," "fanatics" and "illegal enforcement" was to cast their champions in the same light as the bootleggers. Just as frustrating were news stories like the *Delmarva Star* article titled "Liquor Plentiful and Prices Lower" without even a mention that such purchases were illegal. The article proclaimed, "In addition to large supplies of all liquors and fancy wines, obtainable by the man with a purse from his private bootlegger, the market is said to be nearly flooded with Apple Jack, much of which is local supply."

Prohibition supporters in Delaware received a crushing blow when it was revealed that their hero, Three Gun Wilson, was being transferred to Nebraska in January 1932. Wilson's boss, Colonel Woodcock, denied that

Jeanette Eckman and Pierre S. du Pont, 1933. *Collections of Delaware Historical Society.*

the transfer was the result of complaints about Wilson's methods, just as he had to do when Wilson was transferred to Delaware from Pittsburgh fourteen months before. "Gang warfare in Omaha, Colonel Woodcock said, made it necessary to strengthen dry forces in Nebraska by placing a younger man in charge of the agents." Thus the forty-seven-year-old Wilson was swapped for the sixty-year-old General William H. Rowan as deputy Prohibition administrator for Delaware. "Omaha is almost a frontier city and was the former gateway to the West," Woodcock explained. "There have been a number of killings there, these killings having developed from a terrifically bad law enforcement situation."

Wilson had reportedly wanted a change to a larger playing field than Delaware, believing he had accomplished much of what was possible there. He would leave behind, at least temporarily, his wife and two sons, one of whom was attending the University of Delaware and one at Wilmington High School. In one of the great ironies of the era, Wilson's legal advisor in Omaha was reported to be none other than Andrew J. Volstead, the former congressman whose Volstead Act ultimately led to so much of the lawlessness now prevalent in his home state of Nebraska. Despite pleas from local supporters to retain Wilson's services, Three Gun boarded the 9:40 p.m. train for Omaha on January 11, 1932, at the B&O station across from the Logan House on Delaware Avenue. As the *Evening Journal* reported, "The crowd which bid Mr. Wilson farewell at the B&O station, some with cheers and some with hisses, was so large that railroad officials asked Captain of Police Gamble to send policemen to the station to see that order was preserved."

The night before he left, though, Wilson gave his valedictory speech at St. Paul's Methodist Church. "When I first came to Wilmington I was told that there were over 1,000 speakeasies in the city and that by going to the top of the DuPont Building I could see the purveyors of poisonous sudden death hootch scurrying up and down the street of the city carrying on their nefarious practices in open defiance of the law," Wilson claimed. Of the 45 old-type swinging-door saloons identified in his survey, "I personally entered 15 of these places, purchasing liquor in five and arresting the barkeep for violating the law. I should amend this statement for in one of the barrooms, the biggest of all, the Democratic League, I did not succeed in making a purchase of liquor as I was recognized but there was ample evidence that liquor was being sold."

Every one of these old-time barrooms is now closed, some being adorned with a United States padlock and others waiting action by the court." In total, Wilson claimed responsibility for thirty-three padlock proceedings. He professed a tremendous fondness for the law enforcement officials and the citizens of Delaware, and his supporters returned the sentiment. Even opponents acknowledged Wilson's sense of fair play, going after real bootleggers and their establishments and not private homes. They also saluted his policy of rarely arresting women in his raids. Instead of hauling them off to jail, they were ordered to appear at a hearing the following day.

Not all opponents were so forgiving. In a letter appearing in the *Evening Journal* the following was quoted: "We hear you are leaving Delaware with profound gladness. You dirty common whelp. We hope you will be killed by the time you reach the State of Nebraska. You are the most degraded person that ever entered Delaware. You are not fit to carry guts to a bear. May God condemn you. (Signed) The Best Citizen of Delaware."

A more fitting epitaph for Harold Wilson's tenure in Delaware appeared as an editorial in the *Delmarva Star* just two weeks before his departure. Titled "What Good Does It All Do?" the editorial said it part:

> *We believe Mr. Wilson to be as capable a man for the job as could be secured. We believe he practices what he preaches, and that he differs from so many of his fellow workers in that he is committed wholly to the cause for which he is employed by the United States Government.*
>
> *We observe further that Mr. Wilson has not hesitated to enlist churches and associations in the Herculean task of running down scofflaws. Furthermore, he is a man of undoubted courage, aggressive in action along his line of duty, and shrewd as well in preventing leaks of what he is contemplating doing reaching the ears of bootleggers and dispensers of forbidden liquor.*
>
> *All in all, we believe Mr. Wilson to be as earnest, courageous, and duty-bound an official as one could wish for in the enforcement of prohibition. And, on the other hand—with no criticism to offer of Mr. Wilson—we venture to point out that with all the raiding, all the fact-finding, all the tips that pour into his office as to derelictions from dry devotees as well as from disgruntled or revengeful neighbors, with all of Mr. Wilson's boundless energy—we all know that Delaware is not dry, that huge quantities of liquor will be consumed here this holiday period, and that no one who really wants a drink need go without....*
>
> *We enumerate all these facts for the benefit of our thoughtful readers, and we propound the query: If, after twelve years of prohibition in a tiny, bone dry bailiwick like Delaware, with liquor completely legislated out, and the sentiment of a large number of people (on the face of it, a majority) supposedly favorable to prohibition, with the aid of a thoroughly competent, courageous, and aggressive administrator, we cannot stop the deluge, should it not be clear to all that prohibition is unenforceable? Can all the boundless energy Mr. Wilson expends be compared to anything but*

*the efforts of a laborer along the Mississippi repairing a tiny crack in the levees, while a few hundred yards below the majestic river flows over the meadows undisturbed?"*

Harold "Three Gun" Wilson's involvement with Delaware came to an ignominious end with a ruling in September 1932 sustaining his conviction for contempt. At the same time, the search and seizure of the Democratic League was held to be unlawful, and the court granted the prosecution to enter a nolle prosequi plea, or a plea that there would be no further action in the case. The president of the Democratic League, Adolph G. Dangel, would become president of the Diamond State Brewery Inc. in 1935.

## THE END OF PROHIBITION

By 1932, the national tide had clearly turned against the Eighteenth Amendment. The presidential election saw declared wet candidate Franklin D. Roosevelt sweep away President Herbert Hoover in a landslide that carried away the dry Congress with it. In February 1933, even before Roosevelt was inaugurated, Congress passed the Twenty-First Amendment that stated tersely, "The eighteenth article of amendment to the Constitution of the United States is hereby repealed." To avoid the ratification problem in states dominated by rural legislatures, the Twenty-First Amendment specifically called for ratification by conventions in the states.

Since Delaware had no provision for state conventions, the general assembly passed an act calling for such a convention to meet on the twenty-eighth day after election of delegates. The governor, C. Douglas Buck, ordered by proclamation the election of delegates within three months, to consist of seventeen delegates, seven from New Castle County and five each from Kent and Sussex Counties. The election of delegates was held on May 27, 1933, with voters choosing slates of candidates either supporting ratification, opposing ratification or declaring they were not committed. The wets ran up a huge majority of thirty-two thousand votes, and no delegates opposed to ratification were elected. The convention voted accordingly, and Delaware, which had been the ninth state in the union to ratify Prohibition, became the seventh state to repeal it.

Even before the Repeal Convention convened, the general assembly passed "An Act for the Control of the Manufacture, Sale and Transportation

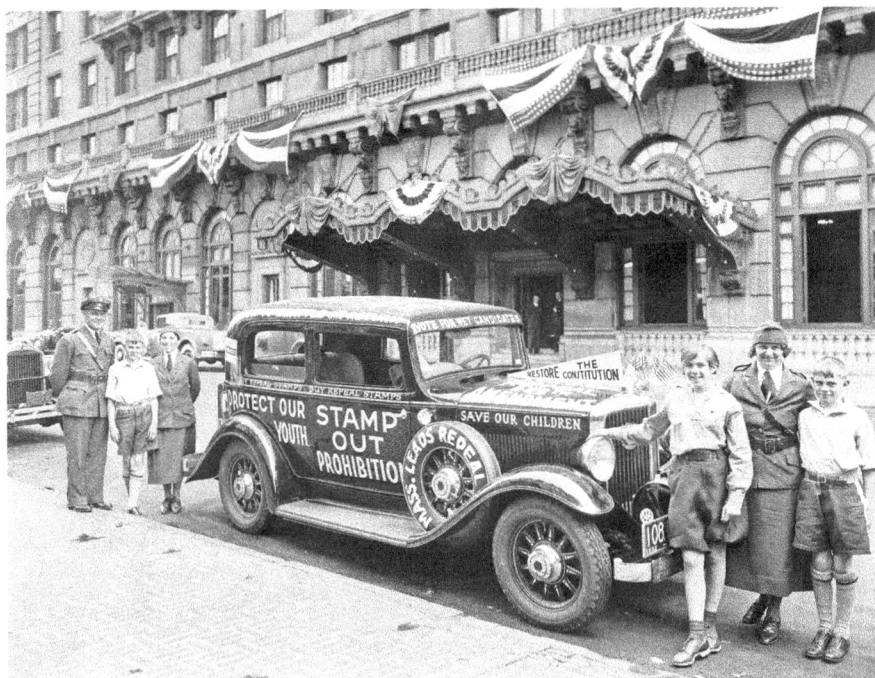

Prohibition repeal automobile in front of the Hotel du Pont. *Collections of Delaware Historical Society.*

of Alcoholic Liquor, Wines and Beer," which became law on May 15, 1933. The Delaware Liquor Commission created by the act was given sweeping powers over the business of alcohol, including the ability to promulgate rules and regulations that "shall have the force and effect of law." It would dictate the "time, place and manner in which alcoholic liquors shall be sold and dispensed," and given the power "to grant, to refuse to grant or cancel licenses for the manufacture and sale of alcoholic liquors."

While the minimum qualifications for those who could apply for a license to purchase liquor for resale required only a "temperate individual over 30 years of age," the commission had wide latitude in refusing applicants. The reasons could include that the applicant fails to provide for his family, has been arrested for drunkenness or has maintained a lewd, disorderly establishment.

Other sections established limits on days of operation for licensees (no sales on Sundays or holidays), times (no sales between midnight and nine o'clock in the forenoon of the following day), age of clients (twenty-one for alcohol, eighteen for beer) and posture of clients (no sales to standing clients; all had to be seated).

It also set out the commission's ability to restrict sales to certain individuals. Liquor could not be sold to "any keeper or inmate of a disorderly house," "any individual previously convicted of drunkenness" or "any individual who is insane or mentally deficient." The most far-ranging power of the commission was that it could restrict sales "to any individual who habitually drinks…to excess, or to whom the Commission has, after investigation, decided to prohibit the sale of liquor because of an appeal to the Commission by the husband, wife, father, brother, sister, employer…or by the Mayor or other competent representative of any city or town."

The bill gave local districts (the three counties and the City of Wilmington) the right to vote against licensure, but by June 6 of that year, all of the counties had voted in special elections to join Wilmington as officially "wet."

The original bill proposed a commission consisting of four members, but it was amended to limit membership to only one member appointed by the governor, to serve a five-year term with no salary. To the surprise of no one, Pierre S. du Pont was the choice of the Governor to be the one-man commission. How much of this bill and the subsequent regulations was the product of du Pont's "paternalistic" approach Harold Wilson had derided a few years before or the product of a general assembly still dominated by rural members who had never voted to end Prohibition is difficult to judge. Without question, du Pont certainly had his influence over the reforms being instituted. "Du Pont was clearly more liberal than many in Delaware on the subject of legalized liquor consumption," according to Terence R. Gourvish. "Given considerable powers by the state legislature to determine future practice, he pressed for the age of drinking to be 18 years rather than 21, and favored fairly long licensing hours."

The first license under this act to distribute beer was awarded to J.V. Tigani, operating from a warehouse at 409 French Street in Wilmington. An article in the *Wilmington Morning News* by W. Emerson Wilson in December,1963 described the scene in Wilmington when Prohibition came to an end:

> *Thirty years ago today there were huge celebrations in New York, Chicago and other cities as thousands toasted the return of liquor after more than 13 years of Prohibition.*
>
> *But not in Wilmington.…It was legal all right, but there just wasn't any to be had. Importers and retailers couldn't lay in a supply until the law was repealed and repeal came too late in the afternoon for any to arrive.*
>
> *During the afternoon when it became apparent that Utah would become the 36th and clinching state to ratify the 21st Amendment to the*

*U.S. Constitution, importers jammed the office of the Delaware Liquor Commission through which all orders for supplies had to pass.*

Plenty of bootleg liquor was available for the first night of celebrations and the orders flowed to cities where trucks were loaded with supplies for Delaware. The next morning, J.V. Tigani put a large advertisement for Philadelphia-produced beer in the *Wilmington Morning News*, stating, "A few minutes after Utah ratified repeal of the 18th amendment a truck heavily laden with Class and Nachod's high-powered beer crossed the state line on its way to Tigani's warehouse. This is the first high-powered beer to enter the state after repeal and again J.V. Tigani leads."

Emerson also related: "When noon arrived and the luncheon trade at the Hotel Du Pont demanded whiskey, the supply used for medicinal purposes was transferred from the drug store to the hotel so customers had a choice of five brands of whiskey or of one domestic brandy." Also, "Hotels were faced with another problem. The new liquor control law provided that no woman under 35 could sell liquor, so many waitresses feared loss of jobs. But the liquor commission relented and ruled such women could serve if they presented written consents from their parents and their pastors."

The old Bavarian and Diamond State breweries eventually reopened in the early 1930s under new ownership. Unlike the years before Prohibition, when the breweries had direct stakes in hotels, saloons, bottling houses and liquor retailers, Delaware's new three-tiered distribution system segregated production from distribution and sale to the public. According to John Medkeff Jr.'s *Brewing in Delaware*, "Unfortunately for Delaware brewers, the new system allowed for wider distribution of other regional and national brands in the state for the first time. In pre-Prohibition years, Delaware consumers had always demonstrated loyalty to the local breweries that served them, but that would no longer be the case, beginning in 1933.... Ultimately though, Delaware's two lone breweries were put out of business by larger, better-funded, and more expertly marketed regional and national companies." Little remains today of Wilmington's breweries. Diamond State brewery gave way to I-95 construction in the early1960s. In the mid-1960s, the Bavarian Brewery was demolished to make way for a public housing project. The last standing remnant of Delaware's great era of brewing, the former hotel and saloon of the Hartmann & Feherbach brewery complex, now houses Gallucio's Restaurant on Lovering Avenue.

Harold D. Wilson continued his practice of raids against unsuspecting bootleggers across Nebraska during 1932, but by 1933, the writing was on the wall. Laid off as Prohibition administrator for Nebraska in June 1933, he described himself as the "maddest man in Omaha" because he was not given time to put his office affairs in shape. He stayed on in Nebraska and was taken to task during World War II by a *Columbus Daily Telegram* editorial in July 1942 for claiming, "Crucial battle after crucial battle in the war has been lost because of dissipation," without producing any evidence of his charges. "Was it at Wake Island that the battle was lost because of demon rum? Was it Bataan? Was it Corregidor?" the editorial sarcastically asked.

Wilson's last known public role was as director of the California Temperance Federation, where his campaign against alcohol was reduced to complaints against liquor advertising. "The printed methods…can be ignored; but no home is secure against the well-modulated, convincing voice on the radio which tells us in a cordial manner of the 'drink that satisfies.' The man who drinks does not need this encouragement, yet the father opposed to liquor is powerless with respect to this insidious advertising." Three Gun Wilson was true to his principles to the end. He died in 1961 and was buried in his home state of Massachusetts.

Pierre du Pont's hopes for federal liquor revenue were rapidly coming to fruition. In the first post-repeal year, the federal government collected over $258 million in alcohol taxes, nearly 9 percent of total federal revenue. As Daniel Okrent relates in *Last Call*, "All this new money did facilitate a cut in income taxes. The levy paid by workers earning $2,000 to $3,000 annually dropped by a full 20 percent in the years immediately following Repeal. But it didn't go down for the wealthy. Much of the liquor revenue was treated as additive, and helped pay for the new government initiatives that began to proliferate in the second half of Franklin Roosevelt's first term. To the economic conservatives who had sponsored Repeal, the combination of high taxes and new programs defined a perfect hell. They had defeated the drys, but in their own view they ended up similarly vanquished."

Okrent also summed up the effect of all of this on du Pont. "Along the way Pierre du Pont, whose personal tax bill in some years was higher than any other Americans, had a revelation: his support for the AAPA, he suddenly concluded, had been misguided. 'I acknowledge my mistake,' he wrote. 'The effort should have been directed against the XVI[th] Amendment'—the income tax amendment—'which I believe could have been repealed with the expenditure of less time and trouble than was required for the abolition of its little brother,' the Eighteenth. Prohibition had been dead for three years, but the damnable taxes du Pont had expected to die lived on."

# 3

# THE COP AND THE INCORRIGIBLE

*I*t was strange the night he died, Christmas night. The boys were in bed and I was upstairs. He kissed me goodbye, went downstairs to go out…then he came running back up the steps and said, 'will you kiss me again?' And that's the last I ever saw of him." Louise Conaty remembered her husband, Wilmington detective Thomas Conaty, leaving home that night to work the night shift. Within a few hours, he had become a tragic part of Wilmington police history. His encounter with a Ferris School inmate on a downtown street that night would shake the Wilmington community and Delaware's juvenile justice system for years to come.

## Forty Acres Boy

Tommy Conaty was born and raised in Wilmington's 40 Acres section on Gilpin Avenue just east of Scott Street. His parents, Thomas Sr. and Elizabeth, were Irish immigrants. Thomas Sr., born in 1890 in County Cavan, emigrated at age nineteen and worked as a textile worker in the Bancroft Mills on the Brandywine. Tommy was the oldest child, born in 1916 and educated at Salesianum School at Eighth and West Streets, where he became a multi-sport star. His 1934 Salesianum football team won the Philadelphia Catholic League championship and Tommy got a basketball scholarship to LaSalle College.

Like many Sallies boys, he had an eye on the Ursuline girls and met one of the Buckley twins named Louise. "He actually carried my books home from school, from Ursuline," remembered Louise Buckley many years later. "I was 15 when I met him and he was 17 and I never had another date and he never had another date. It was a real love story." Louise came from a more prosperous family than the Conatys. Her father owned the Buckley Motor Company on Shipley Street and they lived in a large house at 2212 Baynard Boulevard.

During Tommy's freshman year at LaSalle, his mother died, and he quit college to be home with his family. Louise graduated from Ursuline and went to Immaculata College, but her romance with Tommy Conaty continued, with Tommy visiting her at college every weekend. Tommy went to work with his father at the Bancroft Mills and continued playing basketball and baseball for St. Ann's adult league team, even getting a chance to play against Matt Goukas Sr. and his mighty Mites team of St. Joseph's College fame, when they toured the area playing amateur teams.

Tommy and Louise were ready to get married, but he needed a steady job. He applied for the Wilmington police force and was hired on April 1, 1940. Tommy and Louise were married soon after at Christ Our King Church and lived nearby on the 200 block of West Twenty-Ninth Street for their first few years.

Tom worked in patrol for six years before being promoted to detective. "He worked awfully hard for his promotion," said Louise Conaty, "and he liked being called Detective Conaty." World War II was raging, and most able-bodied men were in the armed forces, but Conaty was considered essential personnel as a police officer and was exempted from the draft. An early partner of Conaty's was George McLaughlin, Conaty's senior on the police force by a few years and an athlete in his own right. "That's why Tom and I had a lot to talk about, because I'd been a squash and tennis player and he was of course a basketball player," recalled McLaughlin.

George McLaughlin was a different type of police officer than his partner. "Tom came home and reported [to his wife Louise] how tough George was," McLaughlin laughed in recalling. "That George didn't take no bull." If George McLaughlin was more a typical cop, his partner was not. "Now Tom Conaty was a real gentleman. He would be good company, a nice dresser. You could send him anyplace to interview the women. He was just different. He really thought and acted more like a fellow that should have gone in the priesthood or become a social worker. Because as a police officer, well, he was too nice a guy."

St. Ann's basketball team, circa 1938. Tom Conaty is standing fourth from the right. Author's father, John R. McGonegal, pictured standing at far right and author's grandfather Mike McGonegal is seated in the center in a suit. *Author's personal collection.*

As much as McLaughlin liked his partner, Conaty's approach to police work sometimes bothered him:

> He [Conaty] *was working with me and I saw some fellows I had arrested for breaking and entering on Maryland Avenue at the Cozy Corner. So I pulled over (I was driving) and was going to get them off the corner plus check them out and see what they had to say. I got out and talked to these guys and had a crowd around me. I came back to the car and Tom was still sitting there. So I said to Tom, you know, I didn't know what was going to happen with that crowd and you should have been out there on your feet. He said, "George, the fellows that were on the corner, why, I played basketball with them and played football with them." I said, now Tom, I just arrested them fellows for breaking in houses. They're leading a different life and now you're a policeman so you have to be a policeman. You have to separate the fact that they might have been nice boys in Salesianum but they're sure as hell not nice boys now. We could get hurt. You're going to have to get off your fat ass and you're going to have to use those two good arms.*

By 1946, the war was over, and the troops were returning home. Tom and Louise now were parents to three boys, Tom, Bill and Jerry. They had moved to new housing on Locust Street. "That was Eastlake," remembered Louise Conaty. "And it was a privilege to live there because only personnel who were considered essential to the war were permitted to live there." Police officers might have been considered essential, but they were hardly well paid, with many qualifying for subsidized housing. In 1942, the Wilmington police officers attempted to form a Fraternal Order of Police (FOP) chapter, much to the consternation of the city administration. At that time, in addition to low pay, there were

Detective Thomas P. Conaty Jr.

Detective Tom Conaty, Wilmington Police Department. *Courtesy of Conaty family.*

no health benefits, long work weeks and little input from officers on work conditions. And no life insurance. Wilmington Public Safety commissioners banned officers from joining the FOP, threatening to punish any officers who joined. Tom Conaty was among the one hundred officers who were given four hours extra duty for joining, and all subsequently resigned from the FOP.

Tom Conaty III was the oldest of the three Conaty boys and remembers a bit about his father:

*I remember his personality. He was an absolutely calm man. One day we were on Governor Printz Boulevard in our old Model T Ford. They had a little black canvas top and I always remember that because we had a rip in the canvas. We always kept a bucket in the car to get the water as it would drip through. My Dad was driving down Governor Printz [Boulevard], heading to Wilmington, and my brother Bill was on the right side of the seat and I was on the left side. Bill was playing with the doorknob and I watched him roll out [of the car] onto Governor Printz Boulevard. It wasn't a heavily traveled road; there weren't many cars. And about a block or so [later] I said, "Dad, Bill fell out of the car." And I remember this very calm man, this man nothing could upset, getting so upset. He backed up the car got out and ran over to Bill, picking him up and brushing him off. Nothing happened to him. He was perfectly fine.*

# I'M DANNY NORRIS

In late 1946, Tom began partnering with Frank Miller. The detective bureau was separate from patrol; plainclothes officers usually worked the day shift to follow up on the complaints and arrests from overnight. On Christmas night, 1946, though, Tom was scheduled to work an overnight shift with Miller and left home around 11:30 p.m. Around 2:45 a.m., the detectives were patrolling Market Street when they turned down East Seventh Street and noticed two boys walking down East Seventh Street carrying a few boxes. Detective Miller pulled their prowl car to the curb, and Detective Conaty called the two youths over. When Conaty asked them who they were and what they were doing out at that hour, the older youth said, "You ought to know me, I'm Danny Norris."

Many Wilmington police officers did in fact know Danny Norris well and with good reason, but not, it seems, Tom Conaty. A slight youth at five foot, four and 120 pounds with brown hair and eyes, Norris was born in 1929 to Herman Norris and Pauline Ziebell. Norris had spent most of his life living with his maternal grandmother in Wilmington. His father had died, and his mother lived in Philadelphia, having little or no contact with him as he grew up. By the time he turned sixteen, his grandmother could no longer control him, and at her request in July 1945, Family Court judge Elwood F. Melson committed him to the Ferris School as an incorrigible. Over the next eighteen months, Norris escaped from Ferris nine times, once staying away for three weeks until he was arrested by Wilmington police for stealing.

The Ferris School at that time was an industrial school with no walls or fences. The Ferris authorities felt Norris was not fit for their school and recommended, with no other options available, that he be committed to the New Castle County Workhouse. While the Family Court judge agreed with their assessment, he had no power to commit anyone under eighteen to the Workhouse. As Christmas 1946 approached, the Ferris authorities felt they had to give Norris a two-day pass because he would just escape anyway. Norris left the Ferris campus at 1:00 p.m. on December 24 for the last time.

According to his attorney at his trial, Norris was "dumped" into the city the day before Christmas and slept in cellars and empty automobiles. He went to confession on Christmas Eve, attended midnight mass and stopped by his grandparents to give them a Christmas tree he had purchased. On Christmas night, he went to the movies, where he met fifteen-year-old Leonard "Junior" Bushell, who lived with his widowed mother on the 900 block of East Seventh Street. Norris and Bushell split a fifth of whiskey, and Leonard told Norris he'd like to go hunting. Norris said he could get some guns. They first broke into McDaniel's Electric store at 823 Shipley Street and stole a radio, an electric shaving set, a battery and a .38-caliber revolver. Shortly after midnight, Norris and Bushell broke through a skylight at Huber's Sporting Goods at 216 West Ninth Street and stole a .22-caliber revolver, three .38-caliber revolvers, an air pistol and about twenty boxes of ammunition. They planned to go hunting in the swampy area just east of downtown Wilmington. "When we left Huber's store, we went back to where we hid the radio, the electric shaving set and the battery," stated Leonard Bushell. "Daniel Norris carried the radio by the handle…[and] carried the shaving set inside the top of his coat and the guns around his waist." Junior Bushell held on to the .38-caliber revolver they took from McDaniel's.

While walking down East Seventh Street, a patrol car pulled up beside them and ordered them to stop. Norris identified himself to the officers and handed his Christmas pass to Conaty when asked what he was doing away from Ferris School. "Daniel told them we were coming from his grandmother's," recalled Bushell. "Then he [Conaty] asked us where we were going, and I said we were going home." Detective Miller got out of the driver's side and grabbed Norris by the shoulders. Miller pulled a revolver out of Norris's front waistband of his pants and threw it on the sidewalk. Miller then found a second gun tucked into Norris' waistband. Detective Miller then told Norris to get in the car.

Leonard Bushell stood by nervously watching all of this transpire. "When Daniel was getting in the police car, I dropped the pasteboard box that I was carrying and ran down King Street. That was the last I saw of Daniel Norris," stated Bushell. Detective Miller took off after him. Bushell said, "I heard one of the detectives whistle and holler for me to come back. I kept on running and heard two shots." Detective Miller stated, "Tom yelled from the back of the car 'shoot him'" Whether that was intended to merely scare Bushell into stopping is unknown. Later, Detective Miller stated that he warned his partner, "Be careful. I think he's got another gun." All of this happened in a matter of seconds, and Conaty was left with Danny Norris. Conaty told Norris to climb back out of the car. Norris did have one more gun in his possession.

Detective Miller fired another shot in the air to flag down a taxicab driving down King Street and commandeered the vehicle, passengers and all, to search for Bushell. "I kept on running," stated Bushell. "The two boxes of .38 bullets fell out of my pocket and the .38 revolver fell down my pants leg and fell to the pavement." Miller got out of the cab at Fifth and Walnut, went through a gas station at Fifth and French and saw the boy run out the other side. He flagged down another driver on Walnut Street and, after a futile search, asked him for a ride back to his patrol car at Seventh and King. He arrived just after two other police cars, summoned in response to a citizen report of shots fired. They found Detective Tom Conaty lying in the gutter beside the patrol car, bleeding.

Anna Bolen and her son, William, thirty-five, lived on the third floor of 624 King Street, over Steinles Bakery. Anna said she was awakened by the sound of a gunshot, got up from her bed and heard another shot, followed by two rapid shots. Her son, William, by then was up and joined his mother on their rear porch overlooking Seventh and King. A man called up to him in a loud voice, "Call a priest. Call a priest at Salesianum." Salesianum School was then located at Eighth and West Streets, just six blocks from the shooting. One of the oblates in residence at Salesianum was Father William Buckley, brother of Louise Conaty.

According to the autopsy report, Conaty had suffered three gunshot wounds, one to his left knee, which fractured his kneecap; one to his upper right thigh; and the third, which entered his left side, entering his left lung and rupturing his left pulmonary artery. This last shot caused his death. Conaty was transported to the Delaware Hospital, where he was pronounced dead at 3:20 a.m.

The officers came to the Conatys' house at 2328 Locust Street, accompanied by Louise's brother, Father Bill Buckley. "It would have been cruel if some stranger had to tell you that your husband died," Louise Conaty said many years later. "Not that the knock on the door at three o'clock in the morning was better."

# SEARCH FOR A KILLER

Danny Norris tucked the .38 revolver back into his pants and took off east on Seventh Street, heading for the marshy area along the Delaware River where he and Junior Bushell had intended to go hunting. All he could think of was to "get away fast." He began making his way east and then north to avoid the police.

"Tom had just been shot and they called in all of the detectives," said George McLaughlin. "I got called out of bed at 3:30 in the morning and my wife didn't see me for thirty-two hours. I took [Detectives] Delloso, Houlihan and we started searching houses on the east side down Seventh Street. He [Norris] stayed east of the reservoir and he worked his way up to Sellers [Estate]. Of course, in those days, it was mostly farmland. He worked those alleys till he got out [of the East side] out by the Fraim's Dairy out there, and he stayed in open territory." Fraim's Dairy was located on Vandever Avenue and Lamotte Street just east of North Market Street.

"We felt sorry for our wives," McLaughlin said, "because Dorothy [McLaughlin's wife] was home listening to the radio about me, Houlihan and Delloso were searching these houses, you know [radio stations] WDEL and WILM had us searching all those damn houses on East Seventh Street. It was rough on the women because she had enough sense to know that every damn time we went in searching one of those houses that we could have got it."

State troopers set up roadblocks at highway entrances in the county while squad cars prowled the city looking for Norris. A pilot from the Delaware Air National Guard had volunteered to fly over the area with a detective operating a radio, scanning fields, railroad tracks and swamplands looking for the youth on the run. "We got some information that Danny Norris lots of times hid in the lighthouse out across from the Marine Terminal," recalled George McLaughlin. Police search parties combed the swamplands along the Delaware River from Wilmington to Claymont, all without success.

Norris made his way onto the Seller's Estate just north of Wilmington, where Seller's Park and the Paladin Club condos now stand on Edgemoor Road. He slept in a barn during the day and then got into the back of a car parked in front of the supervisor's home. The supervisor, Solomon W. Logan, was about to take some milk to the mansion house on the estate with his friend Raymond Tatman. As he got into his car, Norris rose up from the back seat and told Logan, "This is a stick up" as he poked the loaded revolver into Logan's face. Tatman was a short distance away and undetected by Norris, so he backed away from the car and ran to another house on the estate to call the police.

"Come on, I want you to drive me to Chester," Norris commanded. "Are you going to take me?" Logan agreed but said he left his driver's license in the house and he had to retrieve it first. Norris feared Logan would call the police from the house and decided to go in with Logan. Logan made a show of searching for his license, which he had in his pocket, and finally claimed he had found it and returned to the car with Norris. Now Logan said he couldn't drive with a loaded revolver in his back and asked Norris to unload

Daniel Norris and Leonard
Bushell. *Wilmington* Journal
Every Evening, *courtesy of
Conaty family.*

it. Norris agreed. Then Logan suggested that Norris give him the weapon, promising to return it when they got to Chester. Again, Norris complied.

Meanwhile, Tatman returned to the car with a twelve-gauge shotgun and fired a blast over the top of the car. "Stop shooting, I've got the gun," shouted Logan. They told Norris that he was going to be turned over to the police, and Norris begged them not to, saying he was already in enough trouble. Logan and Tatman told him they thought he was the one who had shot the police officer. "Is he dead?" asked Norris. "You know he is," replied Tatman.

Logan and Tatman drove to the state police station at Penny Hill, which was vacant at the time, and from a pay phone on the site called the operator, informing her they had the murderer of Tom Conaty in custody and to send the police. Within minutes, a state police detective arrived and handcuffed Norris. Soon, fifty police officers converged on the site, and a caravan of police vehicles started for Wilmington.

Emotions were running high as Norris was brought into the Wilmington police headquarters. "As I was walking through the hall handcuffed to

Detective Smith and with Detective Rich on the other side, an officer standing nearby punched me right in the jaw," claimed Norris at his trial. "If I had caught you first you would be a dead pigeon," Norris said another officer told him. "Well, what'd you expect?" said George McLaughlin, "All the detectives were really sick because we all liked Tom so much." Detectives John Smith and Edward Rich began a six-hour interrogation of seventeen-year-old Danny Norris, which ended in a confession.

## "BOYS TOWN"

While Norris was finally under police control, the superintendent of Ferris School, Bernard M. Nobis began laying out a defense of his institution. Nobis issued a statement on December 27 outlining his and Judge Melson's belief that Norris had been unfit for a Ferris School program and that the judge had wanted him committed to the New Castle County Workhouse. Two months before, Mr. Nobis said, at a meeting of the executive committee of the Family Court Association there was discussion of a possible change in the Family Court Act to empower a judge to commit certain youths to the Workhouse when they were found not amenable to a training school program. Despite the recommendation of Judge Melson and Mr. Nobis, the association voted not to endorse such a change in the law. "I am now hopeful that the Norris case will force the change," Mr. Nobis said. He continued:

> *Ferris School is an open institution for the training of boys who can be rehabilitated and who do not represent an undue hazard to the community. An institution such as Ferris, operating without walls, should have only those boys who can be kept there without walls. Norris was not such a boy.*
>
> *I realize that human conduct is very difficult to predict. Certainly, Judge Melson and I could not foretell that Norris would be a killer, but the record shows that we considered him unfit for a Ferris School program and that the judge wanted to commit him to the Workhouse. Had the judge had what I consider the proper power, a terrible tragedy would not have occurred.*

Danny Norris had escaped from Ferris nine times in his eighteen-month stay, showing no predilection to benefit from the school. Ferris School, though, at that time was no "Boys Town" and was wracked by scandals of its own making. Ferris had been founded in 1885 as the Ferris Reform School and recently had its name changed to the Ferris School. It was a state-funded institution with a board appointed by the governor.

The same month that Judge Melson committed Danny Norris to Ferris School, July 1945, another youth was viciously attacked at the school by fellow inmates. The seventeen-year-old, named in the news stories of the time and described as "blonde, good looking," was chased up a fire escape, jumped off and was set upon by ten to twelve youths. They burned him with matches, punched and kicked him and rammed a broomstick into his body, causing severe internal ruptures. He became ill, was sent to the infirmary and then sent to the Delaware Hospital in critical condition. He later recovered, but the attorney general for Delaware initiated an investigation of conditions at Ferris with the help of the state police.

The investigation lasted months and, when it became public in December 1945, shocked the board, state officials and the general public. The *Wilmington Morning News* headline blared, "Attorney-General Finds Immorality and Brutal Treatment at Ferris." The paper stated, "The report…dissects the school facilities and personnel revealing in several sections conditions so repellant and sordid that they do not permit public description." According to the report, the master of the cottage "where Negro boys are housed" was responsible for immoral practices at the cottage and had previously been convicted of three felonies. Spoiled food had been served to the inmates "even in the presence of investigators" and "spoiled food, severe beatings and arbitrary removal of parole privileges are largely responsible for the increasing number of escapes."

The report explained that three men had been designated by the superintendent, Reverend Ralph Minker, to carry out discipline, physical or otherwise. (In a previous news story, the superintendent had described punishment as "5 whacks" across the buttocks with a small strap, though a sixteen-year-old boy claimed to have received 40 for running away.) The attorney general reported that the school administration had said the "maximum number of 'smackings,' namely 15, administered as a disciplinary measure, is in error as all of the inmates interviewed were practically unanimous in their advice that many of the inmates had been 'smacked' over a hundred times for a single infraction. In addition to using the strap, the personnel of the school have struck, slapped and kicked inmates."

The debate regarding corporal punishment at Ferris had been simmering for years. In 1931, a case where a father charged the school with "flogging" his son while in its care made headlines. The Board of Trustees of Ferris issued a statement that characterized the action as "justifiable in view of the circumstances." The next week, the former president of the State Board of Education and a former board trustee at Ferris, George B. Miller, was quoted in the *Delaware Star* as saying, "As is generally known I am thoroughly opposed to whipping prisoners at Greenbank [New Castle County Workhouse]. It does not do the prisoner any good and simply hardens him against all mankind. As a former Trustee of Ferris School, however, I have been permitted to observe that the only punishment meted out to some of the boys which will make any impression on them is a good whaling."

As a counterpoint to Miller's opinion, Florence Bayard Hilles called the practice "medieval." She added, "I am unalterably opposed to the whipping of either juvenile or adult delinquents. I think that any parent should resent the whipping of his or her child which is placed…in a public institution." Clearly, the issue was still unresolved fourteen years later in 1945.

Beatings by the trustees, the attorney general found, "have frequently drawn blood and made welts and that the boys thus whipped were lodged in the 'jug' until the welts caused by the strap disappear."

The conditions in the "jug," or detention cells, and their very existence, seemed to take the investigators by surprise. According to the attorney general's report, there were four detention cells, measuring six feet by eight feet by eight feet, with walls of concrete and a hopper, drinking fountain and two steel bunks attached to the wall. Until three years before, there was no drinking fountain and the water in the hopper was the only water available. Temperatures in the summer soared to over one hundred degrees in the cells, and testimony from inmates claimed bed bugs, cockroaches and mice prevented them from sleeping. As many as six inmates would be in a cell at a time, and some had been confined there for 106 days. Regarding these detention cells, the attorney general stated, "The cells… are not proper places of confinement for boys, and certainly the cells and the treatment given the boys incarcerated therein are not conducive to the rehabilitation of the inmates…there is no excuse for the neglect or mistreatment of inmates confined in the cells."

Reverend Minker initially defended the operations at the school, saying he ate in the cafeteria daily and "I know the boys are never served anything that decent people couldn't eat." Although he blamed the war years as a cause for the difficulty in getting proper staff, he said the comments on food conditions "completely exaggerated that it hardly merits any consideration at all." He admitted the facilities at Ferris were inadequate and stated, "We need at least three ways of dividing each racial group." In answer to charges regarding sexual misbehavior at the school, including that "immoral practices at the

Ferris School, where "socially maladjusted boys" receive vocational training. *Collections of Delaware Historical Society.*

school seem to be unrestrained," Minker claimed that there is "an enormous amount of sexual misbehavior and experimentation among boys in schools of all types everywhere," while admitting supervision had not been up to what he would wish.

The board accepted Minker's resignation at its next meeting, and some reforms were instituted, such as eliminating solitary confinement, but it would be years before substantial changes would transform Ferris into a secure facility with adequately trained staff. The cottage master charged with immoral conduct was put on trial early in 1946, but the jury failed to reach a verdict, and the charges were dismissed. Before testimony in that trial began, the judge had the courtroom cleared of all women in an apparent attempt to spare them from hearing the sordid details of the case. Within months, another cottage master was arrested on two morals charges.

What is unknown is how this environment might have affected the sixteen-year-old Danny Norris. As a slight youth, was he preyed on by larger boys, or did he prey on smaller, younger boys himself? At least he must have been aware of these types of assaults, and he certainly ate the food and was subject to discipline, including time in the jug, having escaped nine times himself. If he was a youth capable of being turned around to lead an upstanding life, the Ferris of 1945 was not the place it would have happened. Ironically, bad institutional food would again play a role in his later life.

## WILMINGTON REACTS; SWIFT JUSTICE

As the extent of the tragedy sank in with the public, businesses and individuals began to step forward to help the Conaty family. The London Dry Ginger Ale Company, located on Governor Printz Boulevard, launched the Thomas P. Conaty Jr. Fund with a donation of $100 and a proposal that businesses, industrial firms and individuals "contribute generously in recognition of the sacrifice of his life in line of duty by this fine young officer." The *News-Journal* quickly matched this offer, and the public fund was off and running.

A benefit basketball game was quickly organized for January 4, 1947, to be held at the Armory at Tenth and DuPont Streets. Catholic Youth Organization president Jim McGonegal led the effort to put on the game to feature an all-star contest between current and former stars of the adult league, where Tom Conaty had played for St. Ann's for many years. Charley Noonan coached the former stars, including Paul Chadick, Buck Lacey, Don Gleasner and Buzzy Gillen. The current stars included Babe Nagle, Joe Hurley, Leo Marshall and Slip Gawarzewski. It was reported the game drew over three thousand fans, the largest crowd ever to attend a basketball game in Wilmington.

Over the next few weeks, the Conaty fund grew with many small donations. A total of $27,000 was raised, an impressive sum for the time. The fund, administered by Louise Conaty's brother-in-law Stewart Lynch, would in time pay for the purchase of a new home for the Conaty family on West Twenty-Sixth Street and put the boys through school. City council also passed an ordinance that kept Detective Conaty on the payroll for an additional six months, through the end of the fiscal year.

But what about the police pension fund or survivor's benefits? In 1946, there was little to offer a six-year veteran, even one killed in the line of duty. There was no life insurance, no health benefits and little in the way of workman's compensation. Mrs. Conaty did qualify for a payment as a widow under the state Workman's Compensation Law, though not a full city police pension. On February 19, 1947, the Wilmington Police Pension Board approved a monthly payment to Mrs. Conaty of $14.10, which was

Players from Conaty benefit basketball game with Conaty sons Tom and Bill. Author's uncle Bill McGonegal pictured kneeling fourth from right. *Courtesy of Conaty family.*

the difference between her $10.00 per week compensation from the State Workman's Compensation Fund and the total of $57.43 per month that would be due her under the City Police Pension Act. This would continue for five years, until the Workman's Compensation eligibility expired.

Conaty's accused killer was receiving no sympathy from the bishop of the Catholic Diocese of Wilmington, Edmond J. Fitzmaurice. In a statement, the bishop called on the citizens of Wilmington and the nation to "consider our share of the guilt because of our coddling of youthful criminals." The statement continued, "When a boy such as the one who struck down this defender of the law is brought before the bar of justice, the soft-hearted Americans say 'No, no. A youth of this age could not do such a thing. Then he is taken before the psychiatrist where he basks in the center of attention, and our press and radio blare forth his being there. Other little Johnnies, jealous of the stage occupied by this Johnnie, plot their own courses which eventually lead to such tragedies."

Delaware's justice system was moving swiftly for Danny Norris as 1947 began. The case was referred to the Court of Oyer and Terminer, a three-judge panel that served as the venue for capital crimes. Presiding was Chief

Justice Charles S. Richards, along with Judge Frank L. Speakman and judge and future governor Charles L. Terry Jr. John W. Huxley, was appointed defense attorney by the court, and the trial got underway on February 5, 1947, barely forty-one days after the crime was committed. The courtroom in the Public Building was filled to capacity, with over two hundred people turned away. Arrangements had to be made for Norris's mother and aunt, who had arrived too late to get seats. Witnesses were called to testify for the prosecution by Attorney General Albert W. James, including three Wilmington police officers, Leonard Bushell, an FBI lab technician and two residents who heard the shots.

Jeanette Steinle, who lived over the family bakery at 624 King Street, testified she stood at the window of her apartment and saw a "young man fire 3 shots into the body of an older man" on East Seventh Street at about 3:00 a.m. The older man was leaning against a parked automobile in a slumped position. Each time she saw the flash of the younger man's gun, the man leaning against the car slumped farther down toward the ground. This version of events contradicted the statement by Norris that was read into the record by the prosecution.

Daniel Norris's statement given to the police after his capture was admitted into evidence by the presiding judge. In Norris's statement, given the morning of December 27, 1946, the shooting was a result of a scuffle between Norris and Conaty:

*After Det. Miller had taken the two .38 caliber revolvers from me which were under my coat and under my belt, Det. Miller told me to get into the rear of the police car and Det. Conaty who was setting [sic] in the right front side of the car opened the door and Det. Miller shoved me in the back and I sat down. I then thought Miller was going to bring Junior Bushell around to the other side of the car and put him in, but all at once Junior dropped the things he had in his hand (radio battery, and bullets, one box of .22 caliber) and ran west on 7th Street towards King St., and then south on King Street. After Det. Miller and Bushell had run from where Conaty and I were setting in the police car, there was two loud noises that sounded like shots and then Det. Conaty got out on the right side of the police car, standing on the pavement near the door and he told me to get out of the car as he wanted to see what else I had in my pockets.*

*I had a .38 caliber revolver in my left pants pocket and started to take it out of my pocket, but it got caught and I had a little difficulty getting it out, but after getting it out in my left hand I told Det. Conaty to "Stick 'em up." At the time I said this to him, he was facing me with his back towards Steinle's Bakery. After I told Det. Conaty to "stick 'em up" he sort of turned around with his back towards King Street and leaned against the right side of the car near the rear window and the door. As he did this I shifted the gun from my left hand to my right hand and ordered him to back away from the car as I wanted to get out and did not want him to [sic] close to me. As I stepped out of the car with my left foot I missed my footing which threw me off balance causing me to fall back towards the car which was open. Det. Conaty was facing me with his back towards King St. and immediately tried to take the gun away from me and as he got close to me the gun went between his body and left arm and I said to him "somebody is going to get hurt" and the gun went off. All of my left arm was through between Det. Conaty's arm and body and when I shot I do not believe this shot struck him. I then jerked the gun from between his arm and body right hard which gave me full possession of the gun and I pointed it at his chest and he half raised his hands even with his shoulders. As I was pointing the gun at his chest he struck the gun with his right hand which caused the gun to go off, the bullet striking him on the right side and he spun around to his right with his left arm striking the gun which I still had pointed at him and I was holding the trigger tight at the time and the gun went off, the bullet going into his body under or near the left arm. After I shot him this time he turned completely around to the right and sat down on the running board of the car and the door being open at the time. At the time Det. Conaty struck the gun and I shot him under the left arm, he sort of knocked me off of balance and as he fell to the running board of the car, I fell to and not knowingly, squeezed the trigger of the gun and it went off again and I believe it struck one of Conaty's legs as one of them sort of went limp and stretched out. As I struck the pavement I tried to break the fall with my right hand in which I had the gun and it went off, the bullet striking the wall of Steinle's Bakery and made a noise like "zing." I then got up on my feet and Det. Conaty looked up at me and said "Why did you do it?" and then I said "I told you it was going to happen" and then he slumped over the gutter.*

Defense attorney John Huxley did not try to demonstrate his client's innocence. Instead, he began by stating to the jury, "The state has absolutely failed to prove murder in the first degree, and it is up to you gentlemen to determine in what degree it will be." The star witness was the defendant, Daniel Norris, just turned eighteen that week. Defense attorney Huxley led him through two hours of testimony, highlighting his struggles with his home life. Norris told how he was forced to leave school at an early age and go to work. Having difficulties with his stepfather, he was turned out of his home and for a time lived in a poolroom.

Norris stuck to his version of the shooting throughout his testimony, which his attorney characterized as a "wrestling match," but under a strenuous cross-examination by Attorney General James, the story began to change, according to newspaper reports. "Cringing beneath the lashing questions of Attorney General Albert W. James, eighteen-year-old Norris today reversed a previous statement he had made by admitting that the detective's hands were upraised when he was hit the first time and spun around." Norris finished his personal statement around noon, and "the Attorney General took over and his questions were delivered in rapid-fire order, ripped and slashed as Norris sought to answer." He questioned Norris closely about why he stepped out of the car with a gun in his hand and his finger on the trigger. Norris said, "When you plan to get away and have a gun, you always put your finger on the trigger." At this point in the trial, according to the *Journal Every Evening* reporter, "Norris began to glare at the prosecutor and spectators noted arrogance in his manner."

At the end of the afternoon session on Friday, February 7, 1947, the attorneys for the two sides presented their summations to the jury. "It is only by the grace of God that your boy or my boy is not sitting there on trial for murder as this youth is," stated defense attorney Huxley. He continued:

> *This boy is not on trial. Our society is on trial. If we had better Ferris schools and better institutions in this State, this boy would not be here today. Your boy and my boy had loving mothers to care for them, something this youth on trial never had.*
>
> *I don't contend that this boy didn't do wrong. But he was dumped in the city the day before Christmas, slept in cellars and empty automobiles and, yes, bought his grandparents a Christmas tree with the little amount of change he had in his pocket. He went to confession on Christmas Eve and attended midnight mass. Does that sound like the cold-blooded killer that the state would have you believe the boy is?*
>
> *Murder in the first degree is a very terrible thing unless you have very clear facts upon which to base your opinion. You men have to guess on the state of that little boy's mind at the time of the meeting. You are not going to guess, I think you are going to be sure.*

Closing his address, Mr. Huxley said, "This boy's life depends upon my ability and I hate to close for fear there is yet something I can do for him. God sent you jury members into this courtroom to stand between him and some policemen who want him slain right here in the courtroom.

We are not here for revenge, we are here for justice. Two wrongs won't make a right. I want you and know you will consider this case in the same manner in which I tried to present it."

Attorney General James and Chief Deputy Attorney General C. Edward Duffy made the summation for the prosecution. "Tom Conaty died without a chance in the world of defending himself," James stated. "He died protecting your community and mine just the same as a soldier on the battlefield but Tom didn't have a chance to defend himself."

"What was Norris's answer when he was questioned as to his reasons for carrying loaded pistols?" Mr. Duffy asked. He answered this with Norris's statement: "'I was going hunting.' Gentlemen, a-hunting he did go," Mr. Duffy declared.

"Norris's career of murder was launched with the shooting of Conaty and he loaded his gun again to shoot it out with whoever tried to apprehend him," Duffy continued. "The defense attorney said the defendant has lived in the gutter. That's where he left Conaty. I don't care where he's lived or what chances he's had, this is no case for mercy. What chance did Conaty have? He was shot like a dog and left in the gutter."

The three-judge panel turned the case over to the jury at 9:52 p.m., with the charge to find the defendant guilty of murder in the first degree, guilty of murder in the second degree, guilty of manslaughter or not guilty. The courtroom remained packed during jury deliberations in spite of an oncoming snowstorm, waiting until after 1:00 a.m. when the jury returned. In the end, the jury believed the eyewitness accounts over that of Danny Norris, and after three hours of deliberation, the jury returned a verdict of guilty of first-degree murder, with a recommendation for mercy. If the judges ignored the recommendation, it would mean death by hanging for Danny Norris.

Two months after the trial, on April 11, 1947, the Court of Oyer and Terminer reconvened, and Chief Judge Richards read out the sentence, taking the unusual step of quoting from William Shakespeare's *Merchant of Venice*. "The quality of mercy is not strained; it droppeth as the gentle rain from heaven upon the place beneath."

Columnist Bill Frank recalled the moment:

*Danny Norris didn't know anything about this fellow Shakespeare Chief Justice Richards was quoting. What he wanted to know was the gallows or life imprisonment?*

*But the judge thought it important to keep on quoting Shakespeare on the subject of mercy: "It is twice blessed.*

*It blesseth him that gives and him that takes,*

*'Tis the mightiest in the mightiest."*

*The word "mercy" gave Norris hope.*

*But he turned around when someone in the courtroom grunted, "Mercy? What did that punk of a kid know about mercy when he shot Tom Conaty?"*

*The chief justice chose to ignore the crack. He continued to explain that an earthly power becomes like God's power "when mercy seasons justice."*

The judge concluded by stating, "After considering all of the facts before us including your youth, your home life, your lack of early training and guidance we are convinced that the ends of justice will be met by a sentence of life imprisonment." Danny Norris was sent back to the County Workhouse to begin his life sentence.

The future now seemed set for Danny Norris, but for Louise Conaty and her three young boys, life was anything but certain. "I've always said that I wanted my husband to live with all my heart and soul," stated Louise Conaty years later, "but if there had to be a choice, I could be a father and mother. I don't think men in those days could be. In fact, I know they couldn't be. But I could be, so I was the father and the mother." The Buckley family, her twin sister and her husband, Bill, and her older sister and her husband, Stewart Lynch, were pillars of support for the young family. The Conaty Fund, administered by Stewart Lynch, provided some financial backstop, but it was handled in a discrete, respectful fashion. "They never allowed anybody to solicit money for me and my boys," recalled Louise Conaty. "If you wanted to, you donated money, but you were never asked. That was one thing that our family said."

They moved to their new house in Wilmington's Ninth Ward, and Louise made every effort to be both father and mother to her boys. "I'll never forget, Tommy [Jr.] made his First Holy Communion after [his] Dad died, the year after. And I couldn't tie his tie. I didn't know how to. So I had to ask some strange man and had him tie his tie for his First Holy Communion. I was the best tie tier by the time the rest of the boys got out [of school]."

Even before Norris was sentenced, there was a public effort to change state law regarding incarceration of youths at the County Workhouse. The

The
Conatys

MRS. LOUISE B. CONATY

THOMAS P. CONATY, 3rd

THE LATE THOMAS P. CONATY, JR.

WILLIAM CONATY

GERALD CONATY

Conaty family. *Courtesy of Conaty family.*

*Journal Every Evening* published several editorials calling for a new state law, claiming, "Many of the youths are naturally vicious and cannot be trusted." The warden at the County Workhouse told lawmakers that there were no facilities for minors as prisoners, and there were jurisdictional problems because Ferris was a state institution and the Workhouse was run by New Castle County. By April 1947, Governor Bacon had signed three bills that, in effect, gave the power to assign youths from Ferris to the workhouse to the trustees of Ferris School and not to sentencing judges. Within weeks, seven youths were transferred to the workhouse.

## ESCAPE FROM THE WORKHOUSE

Danny Norris began his life sentence at the New Castle County Workhouse on Greenbank Road shortly after his sentencing in April 1947. The Workhouse, opened in 1899, was an imposing brick structure with barbed wire fencing and guard turrets at regular intervals. It was not, however, escape-proof.

On October 26, 1949, prisoners were called in from the prison yard around 7:00 p.m., when Danny Norris asked the guard captain for a couple of aspirin. The unarmed captain was quickly surrounded by a dozen prisoners and, with another officer, was hustled to a cell and locked up. Next, Norris went to an iron-barred door and asked for the guard on duty there to buzz him in to get some forms. The guard was jumped by eight inmates hiding behind a stairway as soon as he opened the door, and his keys to the gun room were taken. Eight loaded weapons were grabbed, and the guard, now cuffed with his own handcuffs, was led out the front door of the prison. The last barrier was the gatehouse, where the on-duty guard was away from his post. The gatehouse door was broken, and the inmates, with the guard as hostage, were out.

Sixty-year-old guard captain Harry Harrington had been through escape attempts before and knew not to resist, especially with a .45-caliber pistol pointed at him. He had quietly slipped his car keys out of his pocket onto the floor while still in the prison, so when they were demanded by the prisoners, he told them they were under the mat in the car. While the prisoners were looking for the car keys, the guard in the tower spotted them and fired a couple of bursts from his machine gun over their heads. "It was this that saved my neck," said Harrington. "The convicts got nervous and, without a word, ran like the devil up the road and into a field."

New Castle County Workhouse, Kirkwood Highway and Greenbank Road. *Courtesy of Delaware Public Archives.*

The guard fired again, spraying bullets across the field, but failed to hit anyone. The eight escapees split up into pairs and took off in different directions. Danny Norris and his partner, Victor Bryson, headed northwest on foot toward Hockessin, staying at the former Breidablick farm on Lancaster Pike the first night. State, county and Wilmington police were out in force hunting for them, and a bloodhound had picked up their scent, leading them to the farm site the next morning. By then, Norris and Bryson were gone, heading south toward Newport and Minquadale. They took in an open-air movie near Minquadale the next night but for the most part spent their time walking, cold and hungry.

On Thursday morning, October 27, two days after the prison escape, attorney Elwood F. "Frank" Melson Jr. and his law partner, Robert C. O'Hora, pulled up in front of the Andes residence in Minquadale to inspect some construction work being financed through their office. The homeowner, John Andes, came out to meet them and appeared to Melson to be in a state of high excitement. Escapee Vic Bryson was his brother-in-law. "Frank, I am worried sick," Andes said. "Vic has broke jail again and he vows he is out to get me because he believes I turned him in last time. [Bryson had broken out of the Workhouse the previous July and was quickly recaptured.] He told Mrs. Bryson Monday that he was coming out either Tuesday or Wednesday and that Gladys [Mrs. Andes] had better buy me a black suit because I'll be needing it by Friday."

Melson asked him why no one warned the prison that an escape might happen, and Andes claimed his wife tried but no one would pay attention. Andes continually glanced over at the high weeds and marshland bordering his property and said he didn't know what to do. "I know Vic," Andes added. "He'll keep his word or die trying." Melson told Andes to come to his office at 3:00 p.m. and in the meantime Melson would obtain a gun permit and a handgun for Andes. Andes picked up the gun from Melson that afternoon but returned the next morning to Melson's office. After swearing Melson and his partner to secrecy, Andes told them, "Vic and Danny Norris came to my house last night. They were both unarmed and said they were not looking for trouble." According to Andes, the two escapees wanted to stay until dark tonight and then head out for Pennsylvania. He was worried about his wife, left alone with them at his house, and asked if the two attorneys could return with him and talk to Bryson and Norris.

Andes and the two attorneys pulled up in front of Andes's Minquadale home, and Gladys emerged, very much upset. "Why did you have to bring anyone out here," she asked her husband. "Vic and Danny are in there swearing and muttering that you have double-crossed them and they'll get even if it's the last thing they do." Melson directed Andes to go in the house and tell the two they have nothing to lose by talking to them. Andes hesitated but went in, coming out a while later. "Boys," he said, "I thought they were going to jump me for sure. However, they've agreed to talk to you."

Melson told Vic Bryson that they had given their word to Andes that they wouldn't turn them in. Melson's partner, Robert O'Hora, told them what they certainly already knew. "Well Vic, we are here to help all of you. You are really in trouble." Turning to Danny Norris, O'Hora told him, "And you Danny, stand a good chance of being shot." This was Norris's real fear—that any cop in the state would shoot him on sight for what he had done to Tommy Conaty.

What Bryson said next astonished Melson. "No, they won't. I don't think they'll shoot me and when we're about to be taken, Danny's going to stand right behind me with his hands up. I know I'm no good but Danny's just a kid who still has a chance of making something out of himself. So if the cops get trigger happy they'll have to shoot me first." This was said with no effort to appear heroic, but only with a protective instinct like that of a big brother.

It turned out Bryson and Norris wanted to get into Pennsylvania before turning themselves in to protect Danny but also to get word out to the public about the deplorable conditions in the Workhouse, particularly the bad food. Melson convinced the two the trip to Pennsylvania would be too dangerous and, instead, to bring a reporter out to the Andes house to get their story. The attorneys returned to Wilmington, retrieved a reporter from the *Journal Every Evening* along with Father Francis X. Burns, a Catholic priest and chaplain at the prison. After the interview with the reporter, Norris was ready to surrender, but Bryson wanted to go to Wilmington and see a girl to apologize to her for an insult made the last time he was out of prison. Rather than risk such a trip, Father Burns went to find the girl and bring her back to meet with Bryson. The girl, her father and Father Burns sat outside the Andes house for twenty minutes with Bryson until he was satisfied, and the girl and her father left. Bryson now wanted to see the first edition of the paper to see his story in print before he would surrender. Melson and Father Burns left them at the Andes house and returned to Wilmington to wait for the paper's first edition.

Judge Elwood Melson Sr., attorney Elwood Melson's father and the same Family Court judge who had sent Danny Norris to Ferris four years before, was aware of his son's activity and was concerned for his safety, fearful of his son getting caught in a crossfire during an arrest. That same Friday afternoon, Judge Melson got a call from Colonel Herbert Barnes, superintendent of the state police, to see if Melson had any information about the two escapees. Vic Bryson's brother-in-law John Andes had in fact informed on him the last time he escaped by contacting Judge Melson, who notified the warden. This time, Judge Melson insisted Colonel Barnes come to his office to talk.

Colonel Barnes arrived at Judge Melson's office, irate because he said word was all over the street that Melson Jr. and a reporter knew of the escapee's whereabouts and they planned a surrender for 7:00 p.m. that night. Judge Melson suggested they take a ride and see if they could find Melson's son. At Judge Melson's urging, they drove to the Andes house in Minquadale, finding Andes outside armed with a pistol. Andes told them Frank [Melson Jr.] had just left, "but the kids are inside ready to give themselves up." After being assured that the two convicts were not armed, the Family Court judge and state police colonel entered the darkened Andes house. Once inside, the two convicts stuck their heads out of a side room, saying they wanted to see a newspaper to see they hadn't been double-crossed.

Colonel Barnes had neither a weapon nor handcuffs but still convinced Norris and Bryson they should all return to Melson Jr.'s office on King

Street. The convicted murderer and his convict partner climbed into the back seat of Barnes's unmarked police car, with Judge Melson and Colonel Barnes in the front. Once at the King Street office, Judge Melson went out for sandwiches and coffee for everyone while they waited for Melson Jr. to return with the newspaper. The story in the *Journal Every Evening* was just as Bryson had wanted it, full of his complaints about prison conditions and poor food that had prompted their escape. "I'm ready and willing to go back now," Bryson told the state police colonel, and he and Norris were driven by Colonel Barnes back to the Workhouse.

Within days, all eight escaped prisoners had been captured and returned to the New Castle County Workhouse. Before escaping, they had agreed to meet up in Morehead City, North Carolina, but none had made it farther than North East, Maryland. All of the escapees were placed in solitary confinement, and an additional thirty-seven years were tacked onto Norris's life sentence. The administration of the prison came under attack for the several escapes that had happened in recent years. The lack of sufficient guards on duty was claimed and, it was discovered that there hadn't been a working siren at the prison for fourteen years. As far as the food, the prison administration posted a weekly prison menu in the newspaper to defend the type of food offered to the prisoners, saying the same food was given to the staff.

## AFTERMATH

Louise Conaty remarried in 1952, losing her eligibility for workman's compensation and police pension. Her three sons all attended and graduated from Salesianum School. Tom, the eldest, went on to graduate from the University of Maryland Dental School. Son Bill played football in college, and son Jerry served in the army. All benefited from the Conaty Fund set up at the time of their father's death, paying for high school and college educations. Growing up without a father left a definite void in the three sons' lives. "You can't replace a father," Tom Conaty said years later. "It's the little things, like knowing what type of track shoes to buy or having someone to ask: 'How do you put a razor blade in?'"

Frank Miller, Tom Conaty's partner that fateful night, retired from the Wilmington police force as a detective lieutenant after twenty years and joined the superior court as a presentence officer. He spent twenty-four years with

Wilmington Police prowl cars. *Courtesy of Wilmington Police Department Archives.*

the superior court and died in 1982 at age sixty-nine. There were some hard feelings toward him on the police force after the shooting, regarding whether Miller had patted down Norris properly or actually called back to Conaty that night warning him about another gun on Norris as he chased after Leonard Bushell. Former police officer George McLaughlin remembered Miller from that time. "It was hard on him," recalled McLaughlin. "There wasn't a damn thing he [Miller] could do about it; he was a block down the street. You know when you go on [the police force] they give you that gun and that blackjack and handcuffs, you know damn well in most cases you're going to be on your own. You gotta look out for yourself."

More than fifty years after the shooting, George McLaughlin still had tears in his eyes as he recalled his former partner Conaty. "He got killed because he was such a good guy. That was his downfall. He was such a good guy and should have been a priest or social worker, but not out there risking your life with bad guys that can kill you."

It wasn't until 1965 that the Wilmington Bureau of Police allowed officers to join the Fraternal Order of Police. There had been attempts in 1952 to start a chapter to fight for a five-day workweek for officers, but these attempts were again rebuffed by the police commissioners. In 1965, Public Safety Commissioner Joseph A.L. Errigo renewed the 1942 ban on officers joining the FOP at the same time he claimed to support raising Wilmington Police pay and benefits to equal those of the state police. Within a day he reversed himself on the ban, saying policemen have "complete freedom to join or not join" the FOP. According to Errigo, the bylaws of the FOP had been changed since 1942 so it would not be considered a labor union. At the time, Wilmington officers were seeking a pay raise plus health insurance and life insurance from the city administration. Almost twenty years after Conaty's murder, Wilmington police still did not have the most basic forms of fringe benefits for an inherently dangerous job.

Remarkably, Danny Norris made parole in 1962, after just fifteen years behind bars. He was paroled to Pennsylvania and then in 1969 to California, where he worked as an auto upholsterer and finisher. In 1977, he was arrested for attempted murder, rape and burglary arising from a break-in. Sentenced to Folsom Prison, he was released in 1980, only to be rearrested in 1981 for violating his parole in Delaware. He was returned to Delaware, this time to the State Department of Corrections Smyrna Prison, where he died in 1989. Prison officials were unable to locate any relatives to claim the body, so he was buried at the prison with only the prison chaplain in attendance.

# WHO WAS DANNY NORRIS?

In July 1944, seventeen-year-old Edward Krawaski and another teenager were wading in Price Run Pool when they stumbled upon three-year-old John Gibbs lying at the bottom of the pool. The other teenager dove into the water, retrieved the three-year-old and started life-saving measures until relieved by lifeguards. The young boy was successfully treated and later released from the hospital. Days later, the other teenager involved in saving John Gibbs's life was identified as fifteen-year-old Daniel Norris of 902 East Eighth Street in Wilmington. A little over two years later, Daniel Norris would murder a Wilmington police officer with a stolen handgun.

In 1949, columnist Bill Frank seemed to think he had Norris figured out. He wrote, "He is an example of a killer who began his crime career early in life in a bad environment. At the age of 5, he went to live with his grandmother. Father, dead; mother deserted him. He began stealing at the age of 6. A few years later, he learned all the tricks of the streets and alleys, and the backrooms of pool rooms." Frank concluded, "There's nothing we can do about Norris. He's a goner. But—I'm wondering how many more Danny Norrises are in the making right now!"

Tom Conaty Memorial, Gilpin Avenue, Wilmington, Delaware. *Author photo.*

Danny Norris was not alone in growing up on mean streets without parental guidance. He was not the only youth sent to the treacherous environment of Ferris School. Yet he was the cop killer to emerge from these circumstances. He was capable of showing his humanity, like at Price Run Pool that summer in 1944. And in spite of sentences of life in prison for murder and an additional thirty-seven years for attempted escape, he did earn parole through good behavior after barely fifteen years behind bars. He lived for another seventeen years in Pennsylvania and California without incident before being arrested again for another crime.

In a life marked by a troubled upbringing, "incorrigible" behavior, loyal protection by fellow inmates, good behavior to earn early release and renewed violence that would land him back in prison, it was Danny Norris's one impulsive act on a Christmas night in 1946 that forever scarred Tom Conaty's young family, the Wilmington police force and the Wilmington community. For that he will be remembered.

About a block from where he grew up in Wilmington's 40 Acres neighborhood there is a memorial stone etched with Tom Conaty's likeness, located behind Trolley Square in a small park named after him. As of 2021, it has been over seventy-four years since his murder on a Christmas night in Wilmington. He was the last Wilmington police officer killed in the line of duty.

# 4

# BAD CHOICES

## *Murder and Betrayal*

This is not how he planned it. The barstool fell to the floor with a crash as he jumped back from his friend. The gun went off, nicking his friend in the arm. He backed away across the bar with his friend coming after him, cursing and swinging. Three more shots and his friend lay dead on the barroom floor in a pool of blood. The bar full of patrons looked on in horror as an off-duty state trooper tackled him. No, this was definitely not how he planned it.

## ALICE AND FRED

Alice had a rough life, from the time she was born at the old Wilmington General Hospital through her years growing up in Minquadale, just south of Wilmington off Route 13. She was the only child in an abusive household and left it at fourteen to live with her aunt and uncle on Vandever Avenue in Wilmington. She tried moving back home, but it didn't work out, and after graduating from William Penn High School in 1960, she moved in with her grandmother.

That summer, she was dating a guy four years older than her who wanted to marry her. "And I'm thinking," said Alice, "you know what, this will be your way out, away from your mother. So like some dummy I married him."

The marriage produced two sons but failed within a few years, and Alice was on her own again. She was out on a date and they stopped at a diner when she saw someone from her past—Freddy Gawronski. He had grown up in Garfield Park, next to Alice's neighborhood, and was two years older. "He was my best friend's boyfriend, and I was in love with him." He had spent his early years in and out of trouble, ending up in Ferris youth detention center as an adolescent and then the old New Castle County Workhouse as an adult. She hadn't seen him in years but had never lost her feelings for him.

"I was sitting in this car with this boyfriend of mine and [Freddy] came out. I looked past this guy I was with and said, 'Freddy,' and he came over and said, 'How you doing?' and I thought my heart was going to stop." Fred Gawronski was an imposing figure, about six feet tall and over 230 pounds, with a nasty reputation. Alice's current boyfriend wasn't about to say anything to him. Freddy got her number and said he'd call, which he did two weeks later.

Freddy worked at the Georgia Pacific plant near the Port of Wilmington and got off work at 11:30 p.m. He asked Alice to meet him at the Sky Lounge at the New Castle County Airport, and she agreed. She had dropped her boyfriend off at work and was supposed to pick him up after his shift, but she never showed up. Instead, she spent the night with Freddy, talking in her car with him until she took him home at 5:00 a.m. The boyfriend had to find his own way home and find a ride home for Alice's babysitter.

Freddy and Alice began dating, hanging at the neighborhood bars south of Wilmington. Freddy had gotten a job working at a dairy farm around Centreville, caring for the cows and doing odd jobs. One day he announced he and Alice were going to be married on August 5, Alice's birthday. They married and moved to a house on the farm. Freddy, though, had never stopped running around with his ex-girlfriend and pretty soon told Alice he didn't want to be married anymore. Now stuck at an isolated farmhouse with her two boys and a house full of his furniture and hers, she decided to take action. Her brother-in-law brought his truck, and she cleaned out the house full of furniture, taking it to her mother's. "We got all the stuff and got out of there, hoping and praying that he didn't come [home] because we'd all be dead, he was that evil." When he finally did come home to the empty house, he called Alice and said, "Alice, I didn't think you had it in you."

Before long, Alice and her mother were not getting along, and Alice went to visit Freddy at his girlfriend's house in Elsmere. They reconciled and moved to Freddy's house in Chelsea Estates near the New Castle County Airport, and Freddy never left her again. Alice had fond memories from those days. "I remember when we were teenagers, fifteen, sixteen, and it was just something about him that I was in love with him and never lost that feeling. He was the love of my life, and I was the happiest woman in the world to be next to him. When we first moved in there, things were OK. We got new furniture." Freddy got a job at the Gateway Hotel on Route 13 as the maintenance man who seemed to be able to fix anything. "He was the most talented individual. I think he learned everything in jail."

Alice became pregnant with Freddy's child soon after they married and gave birth to a daughter they named Becky in July 1971. But that's when the abuse began. Freddy's violent tendencies were never far from the surface, and his drinking seemed to set him off. He didn't care if Alice had two young sons and now an infant daughter, he was going to hit the bars, and if she didn't come along, he'd drink on his own. At a bar in Browntown in Wilmington, he tried to choke her because he thought she was talking to another man. At the Dutch Tavern in New Castle, he pummeled a couple of ironworkers he thought were eyeballing his wife. And if he was drinking at home or came home drunk, Alice would be beaten at home.

"He used to beat me so bad I couldn't go out of the house for days," she said. Years later, her grown son told her he remembered those days too. "He said, 'Mom, I remember when Freddy used to beat you all the time, and you would say,' because my face was messed up, 'oh, I fell.'"

Freddy's behavior became more and more erratic. He'd go to work at the Gateway Motel and disappear for long periods of time. His controlling influence over Alice escalated. "I had one hour to go to the grocery store. I was scared of him by this time. I had four phones in my house, and if I didn't answer by the third ring, he'd demand 'Where were you?'"

At another bar, he flew into a jealous rage and beat up another bar patron. On their way home, he told Alice that when she came home from dropping off the babysitter, he was going to beat the hell out of her. "I dropped [the babysitter] off, went to a pay phone [and called her brother-in-law]. I said, 'Joe, I am going home and kill your brother. He said, 'You can't do that,' and I said, you watch me. I had a big butcher knife in my kitchen, and I had every intention of killing him. But by the time I got home he was sleeping. Probably in the end, I would have been the one dead."

Her life with Freddy was getting worse by the day. "It was awful [but] I didn't have a choice. Back in 1972, 1973, they didn't have shelters [for battered women]. He didn't want my boys. He threatened me—I had a week to get rid of my boys or he was going to take [daughter] Becky from me. I had no family. The police wouldn't have done anything. I couldn't go nowhere, I had nowhere to go."

Freddy had a group of guys he would hang with at the bars most nights, one of them named Thomas Barker. Barker was older than Freddy by about a dozen years and never seemed to work but always had money. His arrest record stretched across eight states, having served time most recently in Pennsylvania for robbery. They would drink and party at Freddy's house in Chelsea Estates and go out nights and hit the bars. Freddy's job at the Gateway Motel was during the day, but he began to go in evenings, too, though Alice could never reach him there. He told her he was going in to pick up drivers, but drivers for what Alice never asked. "I would have days when I'd get this sick, horrible feeling in my stomach. I knew he wasn't coming home from work."

# THE IRISHMAN

By this time, they had moved temporarily to the Gateway Motel in anticipation of moving to a trailer park in Avondale, Pennsylvania. "I thought to myself, maybe if we sold this house [and] moved out of Delaware… maybe I could get him away from this mess." But Fred Gawronski was being drawn deeper into a world Alice knew nothing about, and she was scared to ask any questions. "I remember he [Barker] would come to the house, and he said, 'Freddy, I can get you a job. I work for Frank Sheeran.' He said he [Sheeran] wanted to talk to him and he wanted to give him a job." On the night of October 24, 1973, Fred and Alice Gawronski, along with Leon Smallwood and another friend, went to the J&J Tavern on New Castle Avenue for drinks. The next stop was the Bali Hai about a fourth of a mile away, and there they met up with Tommy Barker. Barker talked to Fred Gawronski, and at Barker's suggestion, the party left for the Kent Manor Inn on Route 13, just south of Wilmington (later the site of the former Gold Club, Restaurant and Exotic Entertainment).

At that time, the Hotel du Pont was the only hotel in Wilmington, and the Kent Manor Inn would often handle any overflow of guests from the much more elegant hotel on Rodney Square. In the lounge of the Kent Manor Inn, Barker told Fred Gawronski, "Come over, I want to introduce you to Mr. Sheeran."

Frank "The Irishman" Sheeran.
*Courtesy of Charles Brandt.*

Frank Sheeran had a towering presence, standing six foot, four and well over two hundred pounds, with a shock of dark hair going gray. He was president of Teamsters Local 326 in Wilmington, an intimate of Jimmy Hoffa and numerous underworld figures. He had grown up during the Depression in Philadelphia, went to the local parochial school and served as an altar boy at Our Lady of Sorrows Church. After dropping out of high school, he worked as a roustabout for a small-time carnival, experienced extensive combat duty in Italy and France during World War II and eventually took a job driving a truck for Food Fair Markets after the war. This led him into the Teamsters Union and brought him into contact with Mafia figures like Philadelphia's Angelo Bruno and upstate Pennsylvania's Russell Bufalino. Before long, he was supplementing his side income as a ballroom dance instructor with jobs for his mob bosses.

Working for the mob meant enforcing its brand of justice, and he became well known in that circle. Through Russell Bufalino, he was introduced to Jimmy Hoffa, whose first words to him were "I heard you paint houses." According to Frank Sheeran, "The paint is the blood that supposedly gets on the wall or the floor when you shoot somebody. I told Jimmy, 'I do my own carpentry work, too.' That refers to making coffins and means you get rid of the bodies yourself." Frank Sheeran was not a man to be messed with under any circumstances.

Sheeran had become president of Wilmington's Local 326 when it was split off from the Philadelphia Local in 1966. He had his Local office at 109 East Front Street (now Martin Luther King Boulevard) near the train station in Wilmington but held court and conducted business just down South Market Street at the Kent Manor Inn.

Gawronski, his wife and friends, joined Sheeran at a table, and Sheeran had his bottle of wine brought over in a bucket of ice. Barker had left the lounge by this time. By the time Barker got back, now riding in the passenger seat of another friend's car, Gawronski and his group were just pulling out of the parking lot. Gawronski jumped out of his car, an AMC Javelin, and told Barker to get out of his. The two men walked away from the others, had a few words, and Gawronski took a swing at Barker, hitting him flush on the side of his head. Barker went down and, after some pleading with the much larger Gawronski, was allowed to stand up and leave.

The next day, Barker showed up at Leon Smallwood's house and told him he and Gawronski needed to go back to the Kent Manor Inn that evening and apologize to Frank Sheeran for their behavior the previous night. Barker also went to the Gateway Motel to tell Fred the same thing—he had to go back to apologize to Sheeran. He came back several times over the course of the day to make sure Gawronski was going to show. "That evening he [Freddy] took a shower, got dressed, and he was supposed to go to the Kent Manor Inn and meet Frank Sheeran and apologize for what he had done the night before," recalled Alice. "Freddy thought he [Freddy] was bad. He had no fear of Frank. So he gave me a kiss goodbye and said I'll be back in a little while. He only had a dollar so it wasn't like he could spend a lot of money." He wore a white T-shirt and a pair of khaki work pants.

Around 5:30 p.m. that evening, Barker came back to Smallwood's house and said there had been a change of plans. They would go to the J&J Tavern and apologize there. Gawronski picked up Smallwood in his Javelin and arrived at the J&J Tavern around 8 p.m. They saw Barker standing in the parking lot outside the tavern with two other men. Barker and Gawronski shook hands in a friendly manner, and the whole party went inside.

# The Murder

The J&J Tavern, at 3050 New Castle Avenue south of Wilmington, was a rough place where violence was not uncommon. Fred Gawronski was a regular, coming in a couple of times a week, often with his wife, Alice, and friends Leon Smallwood and brothers Tiny and Buckwheat Milligan. Twice in the last month they had gotten into fights among themselves in the bar. Barker was also a regular and was living at the time with the bar manager, Phyllis Holmes. The bar was dimly lit, with a string of green lights hanging from the ceiling that gave off an eerie glow. Illumination from the Schaefer Beer clock on the wall and the Budweiser sign with the revolving Clydesdales pulling the beer wagon added to the fluorescent light that was suspended above the pool table. Patrons sat at the few tables scattered across the floor and at the curved bar. Music from the jukebox in the corner and the clatter from the bowling machine provided the background to the low talk and occasional shouts from the pool players.

Gawronski began drinking heavily, with Barker doing most of the buying. They sat side by side at the bar, with Smallwood on one side and Barker's companion on the other. Gawronski had tossed down fifteen to twenty pony bottles of Miller Beer while Barker was drinking whiskey and Cokes. After a while, Smallwood got up and went over to sit with some other friends near the pool table. At home at the Gateway Motel, Alice got a call from Tiny Milligan. "He said, 'Alice, where's Freddy?' I said he went to apologize to Frank Sheeran. 'Well, there's something funny going on. He's not at the Kent Manor Inn. He's at the J&J Tavern.' So I called the J&J and Leon Smallwood comes on the phone. I tell him I want to speak to Freddy. He said 'Can't.' I said put him on the phone. [Freddy] said 'I can't talk, I'm busy.' I said let me tell you something. If you're not home by 12 o'clock I'm calling the police."

Midnight approached at the J&J Tavern, and nothing seemed out of the ordinary. Seated at a table with part owner Jimmy Fretz was Sewell Scott, a lieutenant and fifteen-year veteran of the Delaware State Police. He had been asked by Fretz to stop by off duty, and he sat with his back to the bar, sipping his Calvert and Coke. He had recognized a couple of patrons, including Leon Smallwood and Tommy Barker when he arrived and had exchanged greetings with Barker. Scott asked him what he was doing with himself these days, and Barker answered, "You know better than to ask me that."

"I heard what I thought to be firecrackers or a cherry bomb," said Scott. He continued:

> *I turned to my left and walked towards the bar. At first I didn't know what action was taking place and I heard the first report. When I stood up I at that time observed the two individuals in the middle of the floor here, and I observed a gun in Mr. Barker's hand, and another shot was fired along with two more quick shots. Mr. Barker's back was towards me. I saw flames shooting out of the end of the barrel. I jumped him from behind and grabbed his gun arm with both of my hands and spun him around. I could see he wasn't going to drop it so I gave him a knee to the groin at which time I saw the gun drop to the floor.*
>
> *I started hollering at him to get him back to his senses. He [Barker] grabbed a bar stool and swung it at me and I warded it off with my arm. I dropped down…and I hit him in the stomach area with my shoulder and drove him across the room. We hit the wall and Mr. Barker went down with me on top of him. He was still fighting. I pulled his jacket over his*

*head to blind him. We wrestled over to the pool table, he picked up a cue and attempted to swing it at me. I put a chokehold on him. He finally settled down and looked at me. And his first words were, "What are you doing here, Scotty?" I advised him he had just shot Fred. He said "Not me, baby."*

Fred Gawronski lay dead on the floor of the J&J Tavern with four bullet wounds from a .45 automatic pistol. Two bullets had struck his right upper arm, one his left upper arm and the fourth his left shoulder. One bullet entered and exited the right upper arm, hit the right chest region, traveled through the chest, pierced his lung, heart, liver and spleen and exited the body on the left side. This was one of the first two bullets fired. By the time the fourth bullet was fired, Gawronski was turning and falling forward. He landed on his back, having made it from the bar across the floor to the side door before he fell. He was pronounced dead at 12:15 a.m.

"I don't remember the time frame," Alice said. "Someone knocked on my door and said 'Alice, something's happened to Freddy. He got shot.' So we drove over to the J&J Tavern and I jumped out. They wouldn't let me in there. He was gone from there, then. We got [to the hospital] and I run in. I said I want to see my husband. Next thing I knew they took me into a room. I didn't want to be in a room. I wanted to see Freddy. They said you can't right now. The doctor came in and I said 'All I want to know is how much pain is he in?' The doctor said, 'He's not in any pain.' 'You mean he's dead?' And he said yes. And I passed out."

# A SLAM DUNK TRIAL

The *Wilmington Morning News* that week in 1973 was filled with stories of the "Saturday Night Massacre," in which President Nixon accepted the resignations of his attorney general and deputy attorney general for refusing to fire Watergate special prosecutor Archibald Cox. *The Way We Were* was playing at the Concord Mall Cinema and *Jesus Christ Superstar* was playing at the Edgemoor Theater. The Naaman's Drive-In featured an adult-only triple feature of *Swinging Models, Swinging Stewardesses* and *Swinging Pussycats*. On the sports page, St. Marks High School quarterback and future U.S. congressman and governor John Carney was leading his football team over St. Elizabeth's at Baynard Stadium. The Gawronski murder warranted a few paragraphs in the Local section, mentioning that Thomas Barker was

Joseph A. Hurley, attorney.
*Courtesy of Mr. Hurley.*

arrested and charged with murder and committed to Delaware Correctional Center in Smyrna pending a hearing.

Joe Hurley was a young hotshot attorney in the attorney general's office when he drew the assignment to prosecute the Gawronski murder case set to begin in January 1974 in Superior Court on Rodney Square. With a barroom full of witnesses including a state police lieutenant who tackled the suspect, this looked like a slam dunk for the prosecution. "When you got a state police officer standing there at point blank range himself, you got a great case," recalled Hurley. For a motive in the killing Hurley focused on the fight the night before at the Kent Manor Inn parking lot where Gawronski had knocked Barker to the ground. Barker, for his part, claimed self-defense. Representing Barker were attorneys Michael F. Tucker and James Kipp.

While elements of the trial seemed straightforward, there lingered a sense that something else altogether was going on. New Castle County Police had suspicions that Barker was somehow working for Frank Sheeran but both Barker and Sheeran denied it. During Voir Dire, when prospective jurors are interviewed by both the prosecution and defense, the prosecution added a question about whether anyone was a member of the Teamsters Union. And as the trial commenced, an attorney from Philadelphia named James Moran joined the defense team to represent the interests of the Teamsters Union. He had previously represented Frank Sheeran relating to a shooting during a labor dispute in Philadelphia. Moran made a motion to continue the case and withdrew after the motion was denied. The question remained—what exactly were the interests of the Teamsters Union in this case where neither the victim nor the defendant had any apparent connections to the Teamsters?

The charge against Barker was second-degree murder. "Thomas Bowie Barker, on or about the 25th day of October, 1973, in the County of New Castle, State of Delaware, did then and there feloniously and recklessly cause the death of Frederick J. Gawronski by means of shooting the said Fred J. Gawronski thereby causing his death under circumstances which manifested a cruel, wicked and depraved indifference of human life." The trial in Superior Court began on January 14, 1974. In his opening statement, Joe Hurley described the incident at the J&J Tavern and the efforts of Lieutenant Scott to subdue the defendant. He also warned the jury about some of the witnesses about to be paraded in front of them. "Some of the witnesses are, well, they are not pillars of the community," said Hurley. "I tell you that because you have to realize that this is an incident that occurred in a bar, not an incident that occurred in a church."

His first witness was Chief Medical Examiner Ali Z. Hameli, who described in great detail with accompanying slides the findings of his autopsy of the victim, including his re-creation of how the shooting likely happened. Under cross-examination Hameli related, "An individual with this kind of wound would not die instantaneously. He would be alive for a few moments. He would be able to move a few feet away from the point where he was shot. Within 30 seconds he would go into shock, be unconscious within 30 to 60 seconds and dead within 2 to 3 minutes." Gawronski's blood alcohol level at the time of his death was .24.

As the lights came back on, Hameli was excused, and Hurley called his next witness, Alice Gawronski. "I was out in the hallway…and the next thing I know they're calling me in the courtroom. I sat down [after being sworn in] and I had no clue what was going on there," she recalled. Joe Hurley told her, "There is something that I have to ask you to do that is very unpleasant, but it has to be done. I want you to look at the board over there and indicate whether or not that was your husband." She remembered, "The lights went down and…I looked at it and it was [Freddy] lying on a steel table, dead. And that was the end of me. I can't imagine them being so cruel." The *Wilmington Morning News* reported she had begun to weep on the stand. "As she stood up to leave the witness box her knees buckled and she started to fall. Court attendants quickly grasped her arms and helped her from the courtroom."

Hurley began calling witnesses to the killing itself. First was one of the owners and then two patrons, all of whom described Barker as firing the .45 as he was backing up with Gawronski lunging after him. Leon Smallwood was next, the first witness to both the killing and the incident the night before at the Kent Manor Inn. Smallwood testified about meeting Sheeran at the Kent Manor Inn with Gawronski, the fight in the parking lot when Gawronski punched Barker, visits by Barker to his house the following day to arrange an apology to Sheeran and the killing itself at the J&J Tavern. As for why an apology to Sheeran was necessary, Smallwood testified that while sitting with Sheeran at the Kent Manor Inn he had ordered a bottle of wine that ended up on Sheeran's bill. Under cross-examination by defense attorney Tucker, Smallwood admitted putting a gun to Barker's head at the Dutch Tavern a month before the murder but declared there was no bad blood between them.

Hurley called the star witness for the prosecution, Lieutenant Sewell Scott of the Delaware State Police. Scott was able to describe with the professionalism of an experienced police officer the events of that night at the J&J Tavern, how he first thought he was hearing firecrackers going off, to seeing Barker firing the .45 at Gawronski, to the ensuing wrestling match to subdue the clearly disturbed and drunken assailant. It wasn't until the cross-examination by defense attorney James Kipp that the crux of the defense began to emerge:

Kipp: Now when you talked to Mr. Barker prior to the shooting did you observe him?
Lieutenant Scott: Yes.
Kipp: Would you say it appeared he didn't have a gun on him?
Lieutenant Scott: That's right.

Even with a redirect from the prosecution that had Sewell state he hadn't frisked or patted down Barker at the time, the first seeds of doubt had been planted.

The third day of the trial, the defendant, Thomas Barker, took the stand, and his claims of self-defense took center stage. He stated his height and weight (five foot, nine, 175 pounds) to establish that he gave away several inches and over 50 pounds to the deceased. Barker testified about Fred Gawronski's violent history, relating four separate incidents he witnessed just in the weeks preceding Gawronski's death. In one incident at the J&J Tavern the month before between Gawronski and his wife, Gawronski "punched her and knocked the chair she was sitting in, completely disintegrated, and the wig she was wearing flew one way and she went the other." The police were called, but no arrests were made. At a bar at Chestnut and S. Harrison Streets in Wilmington's Hedgeville area, a guy brushed against Gawronski's knee. Gawronski jumped up and broke a beer bottle. "The guy threw his hand up, and Fred knocked the guy cold, after the guy stopped the bottle with his hand. The guy got cut bad, extremely bad." In another incident, again at the J&J, both Gawronskis, Tiny and Buckwheat Milligan, Leon Smallwood and his wife and sister-in-law were all involved, with Gawronski knocking his friend Leon Smallwood to the ground and the two threatening each other.

Barker then related his version of the night before the murder at the Kent Manor Inn, one a bit different than Leon Smallwood's. According to Barker, he invited Gawronski to the Kent Manor Inn to inspect a room he was going to have Gawronski renovate for the owner. He wanted to get maintenance business for Gawronski and Barker's brother's remodeling company. He acknowledged that he introduced Gawronski and his party to Frank Sheeran but then left for an hour and a half. He said he found out later that Fred Gawronski and Leon Smallwood had made a mess of the lounge area, throwing everything off the tables. When he returned, Gawronski confronted him in the parking lot of the Kent Manor Inn and knocked him to the ground.

The next day, Barker said he visited Leon Smallwood and told him he had to go apologize to the manager of the Kent Manor Inn because they (Gawronski and Smallwood) had thrown everything off the tables in the lounge the night before. He also went to the Gateway Motel to meet with Gawronski to discuss splitting the maintenance money they were to get from the new work at the Kent Manor Inn.

Barker's version of events the following night at the J&J Tavern conformed to other descriptions given so far, up to a point. There was a generally friendly atmosphere, both he and Gawronski were drinking heavily, and something set Gawronski off, directed at another patron, Bobby Henderson. "So this barmaid was walking up and down giving us drinks," Barker testified. He continued:

*And there was a remark made about this barmaid by—I don't know who made the remark. I really wasn't paying any attention. The first thing I knew Fred grabbed him* [Bobby Henderson], *smacked him on the side of the face a few times. And so when he did that, he put his right hand at his right front pocket, and that's the first time that I realized Fred Gawronski had a weapon. He let this kid down, and that's when I grabbed Fred and I said, "Please Fred, no trouble, no trouble." And then Fred released the guy and the guy immediately went out the front door.*

*Fred was a completely different, changed person, because he kept standing there and he wanted to go outside. I said, "Fred, please sit down." Well, that's when he set down again…then he started acting real belligerent towards me, you know.…And it seems like this incident with this other guy had triggered him off or something. So I had knew* [sic] *then he was armed, so I wanted to get away.*

Barker claimed he asked Freddy for permission to get up and go to the bathroom, but Gawronski replied, "If you get off that bar stool…I'm going to shoot you right there." A few minutes later, Barker said he decided to get up and try to get away. "The chair fell out from under me…just as I got up Freddy grasped what was happening…because he come right off the seat the same time as my chair hit the floor.…He rammed his hand in his right front pocket, and the gun came out." Barker described his actions, diving toward the gun: "I grabbed the gun and his hand, and he hit me in the mouth. And just as I grabbed it…the first thing I knew, I must have had the gun in my hand, because when he hit me I went directly back, but I did end up with the gun somehow…I can't truthfully say how it got away from him."

He continued, "I had the gun in my hand. He hit me again in the side of my head here, and he says 'Now I'm going to really kill you, you s.b.'…Just as he hit me, the gun went off. And I was pleading with him, backing up constantly. I was asking him, please Freddy. But I was scared to death, because I thought if he gets the gun away from me he's going to kill me. And he kept charging me constantly, because the last thing I wanted to do was kill him." Claiming he didn't remember any more shots or anything else, Barker testified that the next thing he knew, Detective Sewell Scott was subduing him.

Deputy Attorney General Joe Hurley now had an opportunity to cross-examine Barker and expose the contradictions in his story. Hurley came after him hard, but Barker had plenty of experience tangling with prosecutors. Barker now admitted that the room at the Kent Manor Inn he showed to

Gawronski the night before the shooting was in fact the local Teamster's headquarters, that he knew Frank Sheeran and that Gawronski owed an apology to Sheeran for his actions that night and not to the hotel manager. Barker still maintained that he never worked for Sheeran. The night of the shooting Barker also admitted showing up at the J&J Tavern in the company of Charlie Allen (aka Charlie Palermo).

Now the questioning turned to the central issue: who had possession of the gun when the fight started? If the gun was Barker's, then self-defense is harder to believe. But what if the gun was Gawronski's? Hurley had to show the story of Barker's was an obvious fabrication.

Hurley asked Barker, "Here is what I don't understand. How does the gun get in your hand?"

Barker responded, "I don't know. I was scared."

Hurley said, "Show us when you first got possession of it how you were holding it."

Barker: "I don't know. I can't tell you that. You are asking me something, because I was scared, practically hysterical. So I can't give you an example of how it happened or what."

Hurley: "You knew Lieutenant Scott of the state police was in the bar.... Why didn't you call out, 'Lieutenant Scott, help me?'"

Barker: "The only thing I was worried about was Fred killing me or getting his hands on me. Knowing how big and strong he is, he could have snapped my head off if he wanted to."

Hurley: "He is so big and strong that you can grab the gun away from him?"

Hurley continued to hammer Barker about how he could have possibly wrestled the gun away from the much larger and stronger Gawronski, trying to get him to describe how this possibly could have happened. Barker struggled to answer, claiming he was too drunk, he was too hysterical, he was too panicked to be able to explain what happened. His answers were confused, meandering and contradictory, but he never admitted to anything other than his original story—the gun was Gawronski's, and he somehow took it from him.

Hurley moved on to the presence of surgical gloves found in the pocket of his jacket the night of the shooting. Barker could not give a reasonable explanation for having them, claiming he was intending to wash a car and his hands were allergic to detergent, but neither could Hurley present a case of criminal intent for possessing them.

Barker left the stand with damaged credibility but was unshaken from his main story that he took the gun from Gawronski and shot in self-defense.

The next two defense witnesses further bolstered his contentions. The first, a truck driver working for Wooleyhan Transportation, testified he was at the J&J Tavern the night of the shooting. "Leon Smallwood came up to me and said I came in there on the wrong night. He said I was just in time for a shootout." If Gawronski's companion knew there was to be a shooting, then he must have known Gawronski had a gun.

The next witness was Bobby Henderson, the patron Gawronski had hit in the J&J just before the shooting began. Henderson, a truck driver for Mason-Dixon Lines, described his version of how Gawronski attacked him:

> Well, we were just sitting there, and maybe it was something I said. It happened so fast, that he smacked me, that he could have hit me twice…I had a big lip, I know that.
>
> I sort of fell off the stool…I was looking down trying to regain my composure. I noticed his [Gawronski's] hand going towards his pocket and there was a big bulge there. It looked to me that I saw some sort of a handle. It looked to be a gun at the time. Tom, Mr. Barker, sort of got between us and made some sort of statement "Now don't start any trouble." I would like to say that I would like to thank this man. It's possible that I could have lost my life that evening.

Hurley brought Leon Smallwood back to the stand to swear he never said anything about a shootout expected that night. Hurley also tried to discredit the second witness by highlighting his Teamsters affiliation, but clearly, damage to the prosecution's case had been done. The two Teamsters had backed up Barker's story.

After four days of testimony, the case was finally handed to the jury at 4:25 p.m., and within four hours, they were back with a verdict. Thomas Barker was found not guilty of murder. The verdict stunned the prosecutors and Alice Gawronski. As she bitterly told the *News Journal* reporter immediately after the jury verdict, "My husband lies cold in the grave because of him and he walks away free. My husband never had a gun." Hurley remembered, "It was, like, I cannot believe this. My whole career was twenty-one cases as a prosecutor, and here was a loss that was totally unanticipated."

Hurley's night was not quite over. "When I left that night after the verdict, I'm crestfallen, the woman I was living with picked me up in the courtyard [of the state courthouse] and a bunch of thugs with clubs—Teamsters—chased me in my car down the street."

After the trial, Barker said he was pleased with the verdict and with the way his attorneys handled the case. He also said he was sad for Mrs. Gawronski and her children. This was not a new sentiment for Barker. While imprisoned before the trial, he had sent two notes to Mrs. Gawronski, including a Christmas card. As he testified at the trial, "Freddy had a small daughter…and I was exceptionally fond of this child. I just wanted to write her and let her know how I truly felt. And I said I wish it was me in the place of Freddy and I asked her to forgive me."

## ALICE AND TOMMY

Alice Gawronski now had no husband, no job and three kids to support. She had relocated with the help of her Gawronski in-laws to a trailer park in Avondale, Pennsylvania. Shortly after the trial, she got a phone call. It was Tommy Barker:

> He said, hi, how are you? And I said, ok, and my first thought is—I want to kill this guy. He said, why don't you meet me, we'll have a drink. And I agreed to it. I'll tell you what I did. I wrote a note, and I put the day, the time, the town where I was meeting him. I am leaving here, I am meeting Tom Barker, if you don't hear from me it's because he killed me. And I put the note in a drawer in my kitchen. And I met him. And we talked. Why did you kill Freddy? "He tried to kill me." I knew better.
>
> I met him at a bar and we drank. It was like he was trying to be my boyfriend. And the more he wanted to be my boyfriend the more I wanted to kill him. And I thought somehow, some way I'm going to find a way to do him in. No matter what I have to do.

Events were now taking a dark, bizarre turn. Just months after Tommy Barker had killed her husband and days after Barker's murder trial had ended with a not guilty verdict, Fred Gawronski's widow was now dating the man who had ended her husband's life. "He started taking me on trips. He called every day, came to my trailer. I let him come there because I had plans for him. He took me to New York to these fancy Italian restaurants with these big people with suits on. I would look around like, Oh my god. I know these were gangsters," she said.

"We were in New York one time and he said something happened while we were up there with my car and he had to get rid of it. I said you can't

Alice Gawronski, 1991.
Wilmington News Journal, June
2, 1991, from Newspapers.com.

do that, it's all I have. And he said guess what, it disappeared. He was seen by somebody doing something with my car. It was like lavender color, a Javelin. I loved it. But it was something people would notice. He [Barker] said don't worry about it. Report it stolen and you'll get another car. So I did. I know he was killing people. He had a gun."

Their relationship was more than a supposed friendship. There were weekend trips to New York and Philadelphia and intimate relations between them. "I played a game," Alice said. "I wanted to do whatever it took to have him dead. Does that make me a horrible person? The relationship went on for a while, a couple of months, maybe."

It couldn't last long, because Barker's line of work meant he was often doing jail time for various crimes. Alice was now deeply involved in his life. She had given him her dead husband, Freddy's, credit card and Barker used it to rent a car. In April, he and Alice stopped in front of a house south of Wilmington on Wildel Avenue. "He got out, went into the house and came out with some stuff. I don't know what." On April 11, Barker and Alice Gawronski were arrested on three felony counts, each of second-degree burglary, felony theft and second-degree arson. Alice was released on secured bond and entered a plea of not guilty at arraignment. Barker also pled not guilty but was put was back behind bars, and in May, he was sentenced to seven years in state prison for carrying a concealed deadly weapon. This charge stemmed from an assault in early September 1973, before the Gawronski shooting, with a .45 automatic on a bar patron. Also, a U.S. District Court found him guilty of interstate transport of stolen cars and sentenced him to seven years, to run concurrently with his state prison time.

Thomas Barker was now in prison, but Alice Gawronski's time with him had painful consequences. Immediately after the shooting, Alice was in terrible shape emotionally. She and Freddy had purchased the doublewide modular home in Avondale and were only a few days away from moving when he was shot. When she finally moved there, it wasn't with her children. "My daughter was with my sister-in-law and the boys were with their father," she said. "The horrible part of it all, I lost my kids for a period of time because of it. They [her in-laws] thought I was having a relationship with Barker. My sister-in-law, she was Freddy's sister, had my daughter. She thought I was in love with Barker and how dare I have an affair with the murderer that killed her brother. They took me to court to get custody."

Alice Gawronski won her Family Court case and retained custody of her daughter. She was not through with Tom Barker, though. "I went to see him in Smyrna [Delaware Correctional Center]. He would call on the phone, I would talk to him, he said he wanted me to come see him and I went down there and it was like in love with me. I said when are you getting out and he didn't know. I was thinking maybe I could make a plan. I could find a way of somehow getting a gun. He was thinking then that I liked him."

Alice had another reason for visiting Barker in prison—the three felony charges pending against them. "He said, 'Alice, don't worry about it. I'll take care of it.'" Eventually he did, pleading guilty to one count of second-degree burglary while the state dropped all charges against Alice.

Alice Gawronski wasn't the only one interested in meeting with Tommy Barker. A state police officer researching cold cases contacted Joe Hurley in the attorney general's office. "At that point in time I was the darling of the police because I was aggressive, very pro-active, going out on raids, playing junior cop-type things," recalled Hurley. "And I was reckless, probably more than I should have been. So Carl Williams [the state police officer] approached me about Barker…and said 'Barker could really bring us something big,' he said.

"So I got us a room at the Gov. Printz Motel, Williams does up dummy warrants, arrest warrants on Barker, goes over the DCC (Delaware Correctional Center) to pick him up, supposedly to take him to magistrate's court to arraign him on these rinky dink charges. Instead brings him to the Gov. Printz Motel where I meet with Barker and Carl Williams and another cop for security purposes." In spite of the circumstances, Tommy Barker couldn't help but gloat a bit about the result of the Gawronski murder trial: "'Remember how I was always smiling during the trial?' And I remembered that. 'I knew you were never going to get a conviction.'" Barker let Hurley know they had gotten to the jury foreperson. "He knew he was never going to be convicted," said Hurley. "At worst it was going to be a hung jury." In fact, at the beginning of the fourth day of testimony, a report of a threatening call to the jury forelady was discussed by the judge and the attorneys. She was a bus driver and was told by an anonymous caller "if you stay on the case, there will be a mistrial." The forelady said she could maintain her objectivity, and the case proceeded.

This was not why they had brought Barker to the motel. They wanted information on other cases and Barker had what they wanted. "What he had to offer was very enticing," said Hurley. He continued:

> *I don't remember what it was but it was about the Teamsters and corruption and homicide.* [Officer Carl Williams was working homicide cold cases.] *He* [Barker] *could bring us whoever it was.*
>
> *Then he got to his price. He wanted to get out of the charges—"Yeah, don't worry about that" type of thing. At some point he casually says "You know I have to work." Yeah, what do you mean? "I have to do my job." What do you mean? "I work for Frank* [Sheeran].*"* [Barker made a gun shape with his fingers and pulled the trigger.] *You mean like kill people? "Yeah. There's an executive in St. Louis that's causing a lot of problems and Jimmy* [Hoffa] *asked Frank* [Sheeran] *if he could take care of it. If I get out, Frank will want me to handle it. I got to do it or I lose* [credibility].*"*
>
> *That killed the deal, as soon as he said he had to work. The idea that somebody could talk about killing…without any emotion was just so.…I was careful to be polite and courteous of what I was feeling inside because—he might get out someday!*

It wasn't just prosecutors who were wary of Tom Barker. His former defense attorney Michael Tucker remembered him as "a very, very, very dangerous man."

Barker remained in prison through the rest of the 1970s, but not without incident. In a later trial, an attorney accused him of dealing drugs while in DCC, becoming the warden's informant on other inmates in return for not being punished for having weapons in his cell and becoming an informant for a former deputy attorney general (Hurley). However, it was a 1980 federal RICO trial in Philadelphia, against his former employer Frank Sheeran, that produced the biggest revelations about Tom Barker's activities. At that trial, both Tom Barker and Charlie Allen (Palermo) testified that the shooting of Fred Gawronski in 1973 was not a case of self-defense but a hit ordered by Frank Sheeran. As Sheeran recalled in his book written by former Wilmington attorney Charles Brandt (*I Heard You Paint Houses*), "The [FBI] agent said they had me nailed solid for two murders, four attempted murders, and a long list of other felonies, and if I didn't cooperate and let them protect me I'd end up dead from the mob or I'd die in jail. I said, 'What will be, will be.…'

"One of the murders they put on me was the Fred Gawronski shooting that Tommy Barker had already beaten on self-defense." Sheeran testified in his own defense at the RICO trial, and in the end, the jury acquitted him of all charges. Sheeran would be on trial in Delaware soon after on charges of ordering Charlie Allen to give a crane company manager a tune-up to keep him away from a grievance hearing. "Allen had me [Sheeran] on tape saying: 'Break both of his legs. I want him laid up. I want him to go to the hospital.'" Between that conviction and a subsequent federal corruption conviction in 1981 about his union activities, Sheeran was now going away to prison for perhaps the rest of his life.

# A Contract Killing

By 1986, Barker had served his time both at the Delaware Correctional Center and at a federal penitentiary in Wisconsin for transporting stolen goods and was released back to Delaware. When Alice Gawronski learned of his release, she again decided Barker needed to pay for killing her husband. "I went to buy a .45 automatic and was put out of Miller's Gun Shop [on DuPont Highway near New Castle]. I said I was going to kill somebody with it and he [the shop owner] said 'I think you better leave.' I had every intention of finding and killing him."

Barker was soon back to his criminal activities, setting up several businesses as fronts for dealing cocaine, including a flea market, a produce stand, a construction company and a used car dealership. He used others, including his then wife to carry out his sales and deliveries and shield himself from direct involvement. But he also worked with a racketeer out of Delaware County, Pennsylvania, to install video poker machines in bars and taverns. And this brought him to a pizzeria in the Northtowne Shopping Center in Claymont run by Vincent Scotto.

Scotto had been selling cocaine out of his pizzeria for several years when Barker walked in to collect a debt. What Barker didn't know was that Scotto had already been busted by the Drug Enforcement Administration and was now working as an informant. By 1989, Barker had been arrested and charged with four counts of distributing cocaine and one count of conspiracy, with each count carrying a twenty-year maximum sentence. Faced with spending the rest of his life behind bars, Barker began ratting out his cocaine suppliers. One of his sources for the drugs was a fellow inmate from his time at the

Wisconsin federal penitentiary, Teamster James Sheehan. When Sheehan and his partner were charged with interstate travel to distribute cocaine and brought to trial in Wilmington, Barker was the prosecution's star witness.

By the time of this trial in 1991, Barker was sixty-four years old. He was described by the *News Journal* court reporter as "a small, stocky man with fleshy jowls and a perpetual perplexed scowl. He has gray hair combed down to hide a bald spot, and was dressed casually…in a sports coat, button down shirt, blue jeans and sneakers." After a few days on the stand, "he looked more like a tired, lonely old man than the intimidating thug he is supposed to be." His testimony was mostly about the cocaine dealing and his relationship with his drug supplier, Sheehan, but the prosecutors made him come clean on his lifetime of criminal activity. Now Barker testified again about the death of Fred Gawronski, about how it was not self-defense as he testified in 1974 but a mob hit ordered by Wilmington Teamsters boss Frank Sheeran.

Barker and Charlie Palermo planned to get Gawronski drunk at the J&J Tavern, take him out to a site where they had already dug a shallow grave and shoot him. But the plan went awry. At the J&J that night, Gawronski did get into a fight with another patron about remarks made concerning the barmaid. In the scuffle, Barker was knocked off his barstool, and when Gawronski bent over to pick it up, he spotted the gun in Barker's pocket. "He said to me, 'Oh, you're going to kill me.' I stepped back and he charged me." Four shots later, Gawronski lay dead on the barroom floor. "Barker stated it was a contract killing, but he never got paid. It was all part of his work for Sheeran, Barker said."

But if it was a contract killing, why had Frank Sheeran wanted Fred Gawronski dead? The only time they met was at the Kent Manor Inn the night before Gawronski's murder. The testimony at the Barker murder trial from Leon Smallwood and Barker certainly didn't reflect any problems between the two. What really happened that night?

"I remember it like it was yesterday," recalled Alice. Alice and Fred Gawronski, along with Barker, Leon Smallwood and a few other friends, sat at a table in the Kent Manor Inn Lounge. Frank Sheeran sat at the head of the table with his bottle of wine in a cooler stand next to him. "For some unknown reason Barker got up and left, Alice said. "We sat there for like an hour and a half. We were waiting for Barker to come back and we waited and had drinks. Finally Leon Smallwood said, 'Freddy, Barker ain't coming back. Why don't we just go.' Freddy said OK, got up, I got up, [Freddy] walked to the end of the table where Frank [Sheeran] was sitting, snatched the bottle out of there, and when he did the wine went all over Frank, all

Kent Manor Inn, just south of Wilmington on Route 13. *Collections of Delaware Historical Society.*

over Freddy's white tee shirt. And the place was full of people. He turned around with the bottle and handed it to me. I wasn't scared, I didn't know who Frank Sheeran was."

Frank Sheeran, the powerful and dangerous Teamster boss and underworld figure, had a bottle of wine spilled all over him at his place of business by some lowlife thug. "The key issue is respect," said Sheeran biographer Charles Brandt. Sheeran couldn't let a seemingly trivial incident pass without losing face in his world of mafia sensibilities. Likewise, according to Brandt, Gawronski had already shown his disrespect for Sheeran. "The meeting [between Gawronski, Barker and Sheeran] was to introduce Gawronski to Sheeran to get approval to do loan sharking among the Teamsters," said Brandt. "Of course, Sheeran would get a piece [of the action]. They had a time set, Gawronski gets there late, and Sheeran says the meeting's off (meaning he doesn't get the job). That's what set Gawronski off."

The two men Sheeran respected above all others were Jimmy Hoffa and Russell Bufalino. And for them, being on time went well beyond simple courtesy. "Russ and Jimmy both went by time," related Sheeran. "You didn't show time, you didn't show respect. Jimmy would give you fifteen minutes. After that you lost your appointment. No matter how big you were or thought you were."

Whether that was the cause or that Sheeran wanted Gawronski to work as an enforcer like his friend Barker, as Alice Gawronski believes, clearly Freddy Gawronski had violated a code of honor. Barker knew where his loyalties lay and took care of the situation for Sheeran. Sheeran rewarded

Barker's loyalty by helping him beat the murder charge. And, ultimately, Barker turned on Sheeran to save his own skin, just as he had turned on Fred Gawronski at the J&J Tavern.

Alice Gawronski and Thomas Barker did meet again, this time in a parking lot with a teenaged Becky and her friend alongside her. "He pulls up and says [to Becky] 'Hi, I'm Tom.' At her age I don't think it had any effect on her because she never knew Freddy and I didn't do a lot of talking about it around her. He said, 'How are you Becky, I'm glad to see you after all this time. Did you get the things I sent you?' She said, 'I got things in the mail. Mom threw them out.'"

The *News Journal* account of this meeting said, "An icy feeling came over her [Becky], and as they drove away Becky Gawronski confided to her friend, 'I think that's the guy who killed my father.'"

## BAD CHOICES

The relationship between Alice Gawronski and Tommy Barker is difficult to resolve. Alice Gawronski insisted Barker never made any advances on her while Freddy Gawronski was alive. Once in prison, though, Barker began corresponding with Alice and her young daughter. Just after the not guilty verdict, he called Alice and initiated a relationship. Alice maintained that her life with Freddy Gawronski was horrible, marked by physical and verbal abuse. She even claimed that Freddy insisted she get rid of her two sons from her previous marriage within a week. He was killed before that week was up. Tom Barker delivered her out of that living hell by killing Fred Gawronski, yet Alice swore her only thoughts were to kill the man who killed her tormentor. She dated Barker, traveled with him to Philadelphia and New York for weekend trips, had sexual relations with him and all the while maintained she only wanted to kill him. She continued to visit him when he returned to prison, though she said it was to lead him on and resolve pending charges against her. She never made an attempt on Barker's life as she said she intended.

Was Barker truly a target of murder by Alice Gawronski or just another bad choice of male companionship? "I guess. I didn't want to choose him as a man in my life, as a husband, a partner," said Alice. "My thoughts every day was how am I going to make him pay for this, but I was playing a game, playing along with whatever he [Barker] said. For me to think back on that…was I wrong? In one aspect maybe I could say yes. All I did and I could have lost my kids. My kids were my life and yet my mind was telling me I had to do these other things [with Barker]."

Frank Sheeran spent the better part of fifteen years in state and federal prisons, finally released the last time in 1995. Health problems forced him to move about with a walker as he lived in an apartment and later a nursing home in the Philadelphia suburbs. He told his life story to attorney and author Charles Brandt, including his trip to Detroit in 1975, two years after ordering the murder of Fred Gawronski. On orders from his mafia bosses, Sheeran met his old friend and mentor Jimmy Hoffa, drove with him to a safe house and put two bullets into the back of Hoffa's head. Frank Sheeran died in a nursing home in December 2003.

Thomas Bowie Barker Sr. relocated to Arizona in 1994 and died in Scottsdale in 2004 at age seventy-seven. His obituary lists World War II decorations, including a Silver and Bronze star but makes no mention of his career as a hitman for Frank Sheeran.

Alice Gawronski continued to live in New Castle County and had time to reflect on her life. Her two sons had both died but her daughter survived. "I'm not proud of myself, of course, that I was that person back then. [Life with Freddy] was horrible…by the time he got killed I had no love for him. I'm not going to use the word 'glad' that Freddy's gone. He had to die so my daughter could have a life."

Fred Gawronski has been dead since 1973, and time has allowed some of the pain he inflicted to pass. Some things don't heal as quickly. "He [Freddy] said one night 'I'm going to brand you,'" Alice related as she raised her right sleeve. On the top of her right arm is a crudely carved tattoo with the name "Fred."

# 5

# LOVE, LIES AND LYCRA SECRETS

*O*ne afternoon in northern Italy, her lover had taken a nap, only to wake up shouting her name. He would not tell her what he had dreamed. And now the nightmare had come true.

The two of them were in an airplane over the Atlantic Ocean. They were in handcuffs, on their way to Wilmington, Delaware, where they faced extortion charges and the possibility of twenty years in jail. They would look at each other and cry.

> *My only crime was having hurt the ones who loved me. I never intended on*
> *extortion, I'd just followed the man I loved.*
> —*Maria Inez Lorenzo de Bianchini*

From all outward appearances, there was nothing extraordinary about the life of Maria Lorenzo de Bianchini. She lived in a modest home with her husband and two children in Mercedes, Argentina, a small city about an hour-and-a-half drive from Buenos Aires. In 1988, she was thirty-eight years old and had been married for fourteen years. Since 1974, the former teacher had worked for Ducilo, a Lycra plant and wholly owned subsidiary of the Du Pont Company, most recently as a secretary to the plant manager.

Then, through a combination of circumstance, desperation, deceit and betrayal, Maria found herself in the middle of a multimillion-dollar criminal intrigue that unfolded across three continents and ended in Wilmington, Delaware.

It was at the Ducilo plant in 1975 that she met Antonio Inigo, a plant technician. He was a year older than she and also married with two children. "Slowly, I don't know how at first, we fell in love. He was tender, loving, played music, flattered me, even wrote me a song. He would listen to me and make me feel beautiful," she recalled.

For eleven years, they stole hours away from family and work to spend time together in a series of motel rooms and borrowed apartments. But they couldn't break the bonds to their own families. Maria felt no love for her husband but couldn't bear the thought of leaving her fourteen-year-old son and nine-year-old daughter. "I was overwhelmed with guilt most of the time. I belong to a Catholic family with strong principles; it was not easy living a double life."

Antonio said he couldn't pledge his life to Maria without being able to provide for his own family first. Though Du Pont paid a decent wage by Argentine standards, about $750 per month, it wasn't enough to feed two families. "I tried to break off the relationship several times, but couldn't," she said. "Ours was a very strong psychological and physical attraction. Besides, Antonio would get so depressed that he would threaten me with killing himself. I loved him. I loved him so much that I dreamed of a better life together that seemed impossible in real life. Meanwhile, the real life was not easy—lying and cheating and trying to keep on living with all that guilt."

## Lycra

For Maria and Antonio, their chance for a new life would spring from a highly unlikely source—the cutthroat world of international textile trade. More specifically, Lycra. The Du Pont Company, the world's largest producer of spandex fiber at that time, which it marketed under the trade name Lycra, was recognized for its superior technology in this highly complex technical area. Lycra's popularity had soared during the 1980s, with the increased demand for tight-fitting athletic clothes—jogging suits, biking shorts and leotards as well as bathing suits.

The Du Pont Company did not disclose specific earnings figures on Lycra at the time of this incident. One indication of the fiber's success, though, was that Du Pont was expanding eight of its Lycra plants worldwide and building a new plant in Singapore, according to Donald J. Gluck, business manager for Lycra. However, he denied a statement made by an industry

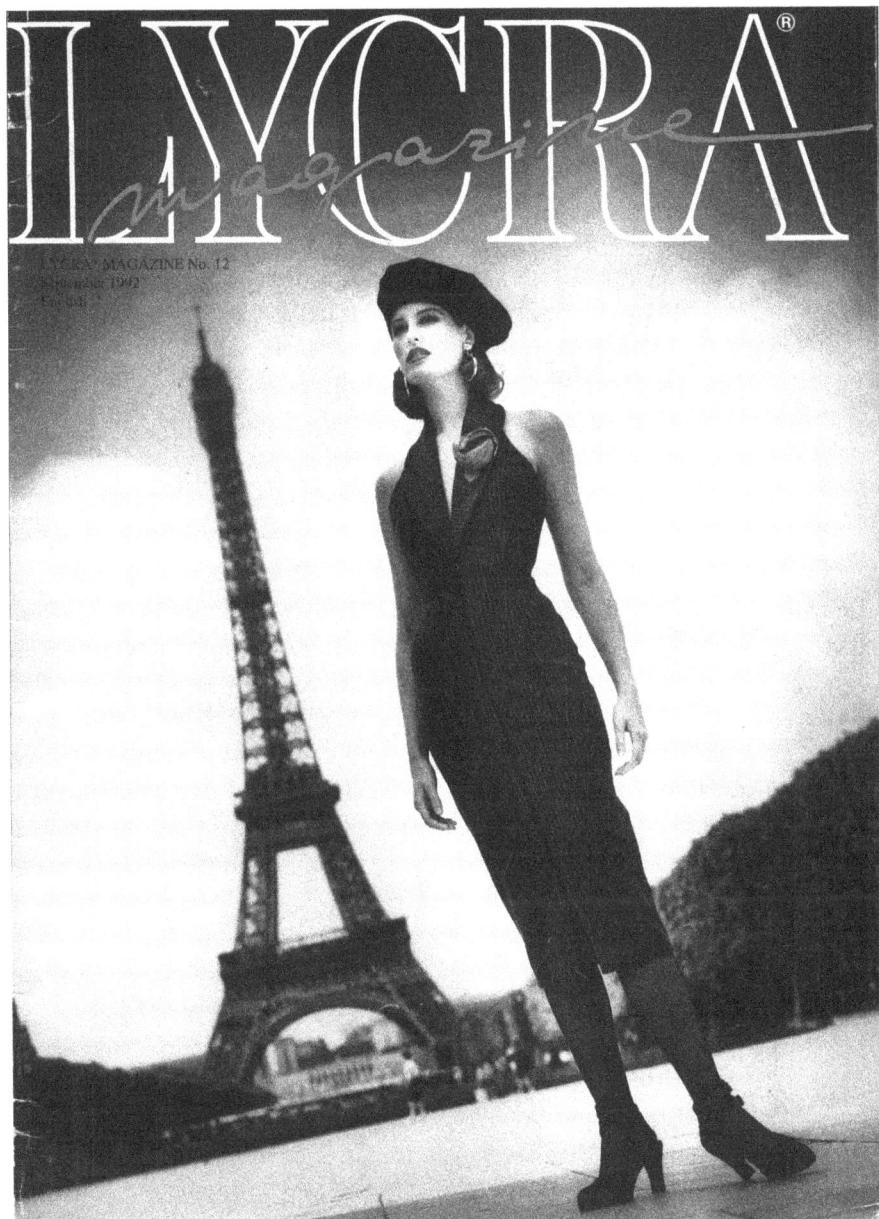

*Lycra Magazine*, published by Du Pont Company, volume 9, no. 1, 1992. *Courtesy of Hagley Museum and Library.*

analyst that Lycra was not only Du Pont's most lucrative fiber but also its most lucrative product in the late 1980s and early 1990s.

Late in 1987, a fabric manufacturer called Lycratex S.A. of Mexico City hired an Argentine Italian national named Bruno Skerianz to conduct a feasibility study. Lycratex was a past customer of Du Pont and in May 1988 would negotiate another supply deal for Lycra to begin in 1989. In the meantime, Lycratex manager Isaac Assa wanted to see if he could cut out Du Pont by building his own Lycra plant. Assa commissioned Skerianz to go out and put together a package based on the best technology available—the Du Pont Company's.

Skerianz appeared every inch the international businessman. A man in his early fifties, he had spent years working for other Mexican textile companies. His stylish suits were offset by a head of blond hair, going slightly gray. "My impressions of Bruno were that he was a gentleman, very sure of himself," recalled Maria. "He knew what he wanted and did what he wanted, with all the money and the right connections."

Skerianz's approach was to go where the Du Ponters were, to find employees critically placed in Lycra production and to pull detailed information from them on the process. These were not patented processes he was going after but trade secrets.

A patent gives security, but competitors can study patented ideas, learning from them and using them in altered forms. Trade secrets are unregistered, private, hidden from competitors and the public. But they have a disadvantage: trade secrets are susceptible to industrial espionage and criminal theft.

Skerianz had contacts at Du Pont, including his two brothers who worked there, Carlos and Ferri Skerianz. Carlos was plant engineer at the Ducilo Lycra plant before being transferred to Newark, Delaware, in 1987. (He became a project manager in the engineering department.) Early in 1988, Bruno approached him about quitting Du Pont to join his venture. Carlos turned him down but gave him some names of people at the Ducilo plant who might be interested.

On a trip to Mercedes, Argentina, in February 1988, Bruno Skerianz interviewed fifteen people from the Ducilo plant. Focusing on production engineers and technicians at critical stages of the Lycra process, Skerianz found three candidates willing to cooperate—Raul Giordano, a manufacturing engineer; Jose Petrosino, a plant engineer; and Antonio Inigo, the maintenance supervisor. Antonio Inigo was the first contacted, and he helped persuade the two others to join him in the project. But it wasn't until August 1988 that Skerianz obtained a final commitment from Inigo and the others.

Returning to Mexico City, Skerianz reported to Assa that he would be able to produce the necessary information and build a Lycra plant for $6 to $8 million. "I told him to forget it," Assa said later in a *New York Times* interview. Undeterred, Skerianz decided to find another textile manufacturer willing to back his project, and by March 1988, Skerianz had quit Lycratex. He approached the Argentine technicians who were key to his scheme with job offers too good to refuse—two-year contracts paying $48,000 per year, up from their current salary of $9,000 per year, plus an apartment, car and annual bonuses.

"Skerianz's offer was so tempting that Antonio had no doubt. It was not only the money, but he also saw the opportunity for a life together [with me]," said Maria.

The three technicians began a campaign of pilfering documents relating to the Lycra manufacturing process from the plant. The task merely required them to go to the plant library, take the documents to the copier in the hall and put the copies in their pockets. The person in charge of the library was also the plant manager's secretary, Maria de Bianchini. She did not know about the pilfering at this point. Her desk was on the other side of the plant from the library, and there was no one else to challenge their activities.

"I was told they were reviewing some information they would need for their new job," Maria recalled. "I didn't agree with that but he [Antonio] never paid attention to my opinion in that respect. I remember Antonio told me don't worry; 'You don't see, you don't know anything.'"

Giordano, Petrosino and Inigo copied approximately 1,350 documents relating to Lycra production. Meanwhile, Bruno Skerianz was busy jetting between Mexico, Argentina and Italy to set up a deal with another textile manufacturer. In Italy, Skerianz found an interested party in Radici, a family-owned clothing manufacturer. Once the technicians finally decided to take Skerianz's offer, they were given the word to make their move. Antonio was the first to resign, leaving the company in August 1988. Petrosino quit in September, Giordano in October.

"He [Antonio] left to go to Italy, telling everybody he was going to Brazil to work with his uncle," Maria said. "I also repeated that information to whoever asked. I loved him and wanted to protect him. His movements were to be kept secret."

Antonio Inigo returned to Mercedes for two weeks in October 1988 in an effort to squelch rumors that he had relocated to Italy. During one of his interludes with Maria at a motel in Buenos Aries, a document fell from Antonio's pocket—a document Maria had typed for Petrosino under the guise of normal work for Du Pont. Unable to explain why it would be in his possession, Antonio admitted to Maria the extent of the document thefts that had been going on around her. Now, with her knowledge of its true nature, Maria finally realized how deep her unwitting participation in the scheme had been.

Antonio confronted Maria with a plan he had been contemplating for several weeks. This was their chance at last. She should leave her husband and children and run off to Italy with him. With the new job with Skerianz, Antonio could finally provide for his own family and give him and Maria their new life together.

"I was confronted with something I had usually dreamed of but was not ready to face—following him," Maria said. "I knew that if I didn't follow him I would lose him. He always said he didn't want to live without me, but he had made up his mind to accept the offer. It was the most difficult and painful decision of my life."

Antonio, in his late thirties, was thin, with grayish wavy hair. A sickly person, he had an introspective, almost professorial demeanor. His only travel experience had been on a business trip to Brazil. Claiming he needed his love with him to pull off this new adventure, Antonio convinced Maria to run away with him. Maria said,

> *Bruno had met with me and offered to get me a job in Italy for the future. He even sent a ticket for me. He wanted Antonio in his business so badly that he did what Antonio wanted to get him and keep him happy.*
>
> *Antonio never told his wife he was leaving her. He was away just because of a new job, and the family would remain behind. At that moment my husband and I were having serious relationship problems and I wanted to get away from that. I told my husband I needed some time alone, that I had been offered a job abroad and I would come back and set things straight later on.*
>
> *I lied. I didn't have the courage to tell him about Antonio. He did not suspect or didn't want to, I don't know.*
>
> *Before my departure I told my parents and sisters about Antonio and my decision. They were hurt and astonished and tried to change my mind, but no way. I told them I would write or call my husband later.*
>
> *I finally talked and told the truth to my husband just before leaving; so much pain—but I just wanted to go to Antonio.*

*I went for 10 days to Buenos Aires on vacation, then sent in my resignation papers. I told him* [Jorge Charre, her boss] *I hadn't taken anything, that he could trust me, that I hadn't done anything....I don't know why I told him that.*

# ITALY

On November 7, 1988, Maria traveled alone from Buenos Aires to Madrid and then caught a connecting flight to Milan to join Antonio. Giordano and Petrosino soon followed, and Skerianz had them and their families set up in hotels in Clusone, near Bergamo in northern Italy.

Giordano, Petrosino and Inigo were being paid by the PNB Company, a partnership owned by Pepo Casuchi, Nando Rivo and Bruno Skerianz. Their two-year contracts put them at Skerianz's disposal to work on the development of a new Lycra plant. They spent their days in the offices of Noi Engineering, a Radici affiliate, making calculations and plans to establish the new plant that would give Radici the production capability to take on Du Pont.

The Du Pont Company had become aware of these developments. After Skerianz approached his brother Carlos about joining the venture with Assa, Carlos told his older brother Ferri, Du Pont's vice president of manufacturing in Argentina. Ferri advised Carlos to tell other Du Pont officials about Bruno's offer.

When Salim Ibrahim, then Du Pont's Lycra worldwide business director, first learned about Bruno's plans to build a spandex plant, he was not overly concerned. At that time, it appeared to be just another competitor. Still, he decided to send Lee Miller, the director of operations in Mexico, to talk with Assa in Mexico City. Assa confirmed some of the rumors about Bruno Skerianz and said he might have some other information that could be of interest to Du Pont.

On November 10 and 11, 1988, Assa was in Wilmington, Delaware, at Du Pont's invitation to meet with Ibrahim and his boss, Paul Gillease, director of Du Pont's textile division. Assa reported to Ibrahim and Gillease that Skerianz had the plans, the people and the technology to build not just a spandex plant but also what would essentially be an unauthorized Lycra plant that would be using proprietary information from Du Pont. He said Skerianz was negotiating with the Radici family in Italy to sell the technology and help them build a Lycra plant in Milan. Assa also claimed that he could put a stop to these plans if Du Pont made some "accommodations." For $20 million, Assa said, Du Pont could put to rest a trade name dispute it had been having with Assa's Lycratex company and get all of the Lycra information back from Skerianz, thus stopping the new Lycra plant.

Du Pont decided that Assa wasn't the one with the goods, so it bypassed him and focused instead on Skerianz and Radici. Shortly before Thanksgiving, the Du Pont Company notified the FBI, alerting them about possible criminal activity. Based on the available information, though, the FBI declined to begin an official investigation.

Skerianz continued his negotiations with Gianni and Fausto Radici, but now Du Pont was also talking to them about their Lycra needs. At this time, Du Pont pressed Bruno's brother Ferri into service. Ferri was asked to call his brother Bruno in Italy and persuade him to come to the states for a talk. When Ferri told Bruno some of what had transpired with Assa, Bruno said, "For $10 million, I'll talk to anyone."

By the first week in December, Radici had informed Skerianz that they would not be going ahead with their plans for a Lycra plant. Skerianz told the technicians that the Radici deal was on hold, but he was marketing the deal to other manufacturers. In the meantime, they could take two or three weeks off for the holidays before reporting back to work. Skerianz told them he was returning to Mexico to take a holiday cruise with his family.

Instead, on December 20, 1988, Bruno Skerianz followed up on the Du Pont invitation to come to Wilmington and discuss his plans. Skerianz, accompanied by a Washington, D.C., lawyer, met with Gillease and Ibrahim in the Du Pont offices. This was the first of more than twenty meetings and phone conversations over the next few weeks. All of the meetings were secretly taped, first by Du Pont and then by the FBI, which became involved in the case within two weeks of that first meeting.

The tapes show that the December 20 meeting was conducted with an air of civility, even collegiality, that would mark all of these negotiations. It sounded like a meeting among old business partners, interrupted occasionally by good-natured laughter and small talk.

Gillease and Ibrahim began the meeting by laying out what they knew about Skerianz's activities, most of which they had heard from Assa, Skerianz's former employer. As the two Du Pont officials tried to pinpoint exactly what information Skerianz had in his possession, Skerianz parried with little deceptions and feints. He first denied ever being in Mercedes, Argentina, for any reason, much less to hire away Du Pont employees. He said he had no Du Pont documents under his control and that the three technicians who had resigned from Du Pont were not in his employ.

Skerianz wanted to discuss an arrangement where Du Pont merely paid him to not build a competing spandex plant, but that was not Du Pont's plan. Gillease and Ibrahim kept narrowing the focus of the discussion. Gillease at one point said, "We have pretty good evidence that they have documents, OK…they have our processes, our charts, our temperatures."

Ibrahim finally summed up the company position by saying, "I guess we're discussing perhaps a potential agreement…but we're interested really in protecting technology that is Du Pont's. If somebody wants to build a plant based on somebody else's technology, that's their business."

Without admitting anything had been stolen, Skerianz began discussing possible indemnity for the technicians. Then Skerianz asked if Assa had ever mentioned a figure for this "accommodation." Gillease said Assa had said it could be $20 million, perhaps $10 million for the trade name and $10 million for the information. Skerianz stalled a bit, commenting on his expenditures and minimum profit he expected from his venture. When pressed, he said $10 million was his range. Then he asked, "And I do not know, maybe you can help me by telling me how much this would affect Du Pont…how much Du Pont is willing to expend to get rid of this kind of problem."

Gillease and Gilliam would not bite. They weren't going to bid up the extortion attempt, and they weren't going to be diverted from the task at hand. They continually dismissed the knowledge the technicians might have retained in their heads, focusing instead on the physical evidence— the stolen documents.

Perhaps sensing the box he was being put in, to produce the stolen documents or forego the deal, Skerianz tried one more time to divert the discussion. "Let's assume no one single document…has been taken from the library," Skerianz said. "Let's assume this. [Are] you still interested in a way to stop continuing our collaboration with Radici?" But Ibrahim would have none of that. "We are only interested in getting the knowledge that belongs to Du Pont," he said.

Any prudent person would wonder how Skerianz could think he would get away with a scheme to sell back to Du Pont documents stolen from them. He was setting himself up for a variety of criminal charges and trying to muscle millions of dollars out of a company that presumably would take every possible step to protect itself.

One attorney who would later represent Antonio Inigo speculated that Skerianz had simply convinced himself that this was how business was done.

There were meetings, there were lawyers, there were discussions, there were all the trappings of a legitimate business deal. Perhaps Skerianz was too cocky, this attorney said, to "see the train coming." Maybe he conned himself into believing the scheme would work.

At any rate, the trap was set. Du Pont would force Skerianz to produce the physical evidence to get his $10 million. Not once was the word *extortion* used, nor did Du Pont ever betray a reluctance to ante up for the return of the documents. So subtle were the negotiations that Skerianz's attorney did not realize what was going on until it was too late. Within days after the meeting, Gillease received a call from Skerianz's attorney. The attorney said he believed Skerianz was attempting to extort money from Du Pont, and he was withdrawing as counsel for that reason.

Back in Italy, Maria was discovering the man she had loved in Argentina was not the same man she was living with in Italy. She recalled:

> *Bruno and Antonio had become very close, they were always together. When I arrived I felt, in a way, I was interfering. We lived in hotels for three months. Antonio had his own car, his salary was plenty—he would send $1,000 a month to his family in Argentina. But here I didn't have any money of my own. I had to ask for everything.*
>
> *We would travel by car, go shopping in the free time. But I was alone most of the time in a hotel room watching TV. I was overwhelmed with guilt and pain for having left my kids behind. I would cry frequently, and Antonio didn't like that. He said that I was getting on his nerves.*
>
> *I wasn't any longer the Maria he knew. My self-esteem was low; I felt I had left everything behind that made me strong. Antonio would get angry at my being sad and depressed. He was different than the man I knew, also. He seemed far from me and extremely jealous.*
>
> *For Christmas, Antonio asked Bruno for a plane ticket and went to visit his family in Argentina. I didn't want to be left alone. I couldn't just put up with it, but I tried to understand. I even helped him with his Christmas shopping. I remained alone in the hotel room for 15 days. He never called. Only the Giordanos made it bearable for me.*
>
> *Antonio came back, but hadn't had the courage to tell his wife the truth about us. [Later] remembering all this, I get angry at myself; how could I be so blind and stupid. But I loved him and had left everything to be there with him. I had nothing and nobody left but him, or whatever he wanted to give me.*

On January 6, 1989, Salim Ibrahim flew to Italy to conclude negotiations with the Radici Company. Now that the question of Radici's use of proprietary information was eliminated, Du Pont and Radici could conduct normal business relations. Du Pont agreed to sell Lycra to Radici—small amounts by Du Pont standards—at large customer discount rates. This gave Radici the alternative to manufacture its own Lycra yarn. Du Pont thus had successfully cut off Skerianz from building a competing Lycra plant with the stolen documents this time but still did not have the documents.

On January 9, Bruno Skerianz again came to Wilmington to further discuss arrangements with Du Pont. Two new players were introduced at this meeting held at the Hotel du Pont—Skerianz's new attorney from New York, Marvin Gersten, and FBI special agent Robert Rush, playing the part of a Du Pont contract administrator named Robert Huie.

After some initial maneuvering, Gersten said Du Pont should assume Skerianz had the proprietary information and the three technicians in his possession and control. While Skerianz promised he would deliver "no compete" agreements from the technicians, it was increasingly evident that Du Pont was concerned primarily about the documents.

Gillease insisted on inspecting the documents before signing any agreements. He wanted the documents brought to the United States, but Gersten and Skerianz refused. To keep the deal alive, Du Pont finally agreed that Du Pont officials would travel to Italy to review the documents before the agreement was finalized. Gersten returned to New York and discussed the Du Pont negotiations with his partners. In a nervous, stammering voice, Gersten then called Gillease at Du Pont and attempted to create a legal safety net for himself. He asked Gillease point blank if this was a matter of extortion, commenting that he wanted out if it was. Gillease was evasive, never directly answering the question. Instead, he just reemphasized that he wanted Du Pont's property back. Gersten said that he could draft such an agreement.

As the weeks progressed, Maria was becoming increasingly depressed with her situation. She said, "I would call my parents in Argentina sometimes. My husband and kids wouldn't talk to me. Antonio would call his family every Friday. In Mercedes, everybody gossiped about our being together, so his wife always asked. Antonio consistently denied my presence. I was there and could hear him. I would ask, 'Are you going to tell her?' He would answer, 'Not now, later; I don't know, I don't want to lose my kids and suffer, like you.'"

In January, Maria and Antonio found that they and the others were being moved from their hotels to much less spacious apartments. Instead of going to work every day at Radici, they were now going to Pepo Casuchi's villa in Oggiono to do their work. The jobs themselves were also changing. The preparation to turn the documents into working plans for a new plant now became busy work, collating and copying all the documents for no apparent reason. The paychecks from PNB continued to come in, so they continued to trust Skerianz.

On January 27, Ibrahim, Jacob Kleinschuster, technical director for Du Pont's Textiles Division and Jorge Charre, Ducilo plant superintendent, traveled to Milan to review the documents. Skerianz and two of his security men, as described by court documents, led Ibrahim and his associates to a basement room of the Milan Hilton Hotel, and for the next several hours, the Du Pont officials pored over the approximately 1,350 documents. Here Ibrahim saw everything from blueprints for construction of Lycra manufacturing plants to the specific processes for manufacturing Lycra. Skerianz made no effort to disguise the source of the documents, which in many cases had the Du Pont name or trademark on them. Ibrahim, one of the early developers of the Lycra technology, even found documents he had originated during past years of research. In fact, some papers contained Ibrahim's and Charre's own handwritten notes.

This was the mother lode. In the right hands, this information would allow a company to duplicate the entire Lycra manufacturing process. And plenty of evidence tied all of this information back to Du Pont's plant in Mercedes.

Gillease telephoned Skerianz in Italy on January 30, advising him the Du Pont Company was prepared to exchange $10 million for the return of the documents. This was relayed to Gersten in New York, who then called Gillease to work out the final exchange terms. Gillease made one more attempt to force Skerianz to bring the documents to the United States, but Gersten balked. Saying such a proposal was a "dealbreaker," Gersten insisted the exchange take place in Europe.

Skerianz kept Maria and the others in the dark about his negotiations with Du Pont right through January and February, until one week before the exchange was scheduled to take place. On February 20, Skerianz, supposedly coming back from Mexico, called for Antonio to fetch him at the airport. Later, in Antonio and Maria's apartment, Skerianz gave them the big news: "Bruno said, 'Well, I have good news, I sold the project. Guess to whom?' And I said, just to say something very funny, 'Yes, to Du Pont!' And he said, 'Yes.' And I was astonished that I just said, 'What?'"

Still, Skerianz reassured them that everything was legal and aboveboard. He said he would take care of them, though they would have to sign

*Du Pont Magazine*, volume 73, no. 3, 1979. *Courtesy of Hagley Museum and Library.*

agreements preventing them from being employed for the next five years at the one thing they knew how to do—make Lycra.

No mention was made of the $10 million payment; instead, Skerianz told them they were each to get a $50,000 payment to buy them out of their contract with PNB. In addition, they would receive another $50,000 from PNB in five years for agreeing to sign the "no compete" agreement. They were all to go to Geneva the following week to sign the paperwork with Du Pont to complete the deal. Giordano, Petrosino, Maria and Antonio had burned their bridges behind them and saw no alternative but to follow Skerianz's directions. But they were extremely wary about facing their former employer.

# ARREST

Skerianz was taking extra precautions to make sure Du Pont fulfilled its bargain and that his accomplices would not know the extent of the deal. Skerianz hired a Swiss attorney named Allen Farina to oversee the exchange, scheduled to take place at the Citibank offices in Geneva on February 27. The Swiss attorney in turn employed a retired Geneva police officer as a private investigator to assist him. Bruno had also arranged the sequencing of the settlement so that the others would meet with the Du Pont officials first, attest to their agreements and then leave. That way, they would be out of the room before the certified check for $10 million was handed over.

Du Pont and the FBI also made plans for the proposed settlement. For two months, Gillease, Ibrahim and the FBI conducted exhaustive negotiations to draw up the agreements with Skerianz—agreements they never intended to sign. By February 15, the FBI had enough evidence to have the U.S. District Court in Wilmington issue provisional arrest warrants for Skerianz, Giordano, Petrosino, Antonio Inigo and Maria de Bianchini. Arrangements were made with the Swiss police, who adopted the warrants sent by the U.S Attorney's Office, and Citibank to make the arrests in the Citibank offices in Geneva once the documents were turned over.

The final piece of evidence was delivered to Du Pont's offices on February 22, when Skerianz's attorney submitted the settlement agreement. The agreement stated, in part, that Skerianz, the technicians and Maria de Bianchini "have certain documents in their possession and control relating to the Technology…which have been inspected by representatives of Du Pont."

With this agreement in hand, Ibrahim and FBI investigator Michael Kirchenbauer flew to Geneva to close the trap.

Maria and the technicians had resigned themselves to this new state of affairs and began making plans for the future. Giordano and Petrosino intended to stay in Italy and work for Skerianz's Italian partners. Antonio and Maria were going to follow Skerianz back to Mexico, where Antonio would work for Lycratex while Maria worked for Bruno's wife Sylvia Skerianz's travel agency.

Maria recalled, "One afternoon, I think he [Antonio] was taking a nap, when he woke up shouting my name. I was around the house, and I went there and I said, 'What's wrong? Don't you feel well? What's happening?' He said, 'I'm OK, I'm OK.' 'But what's wrong? Why were you shouting!' He said, 'Do me a favor, please. On Monday, when we go up to Geneva, don't put on that purple sweater.' 'Why not,' I said. And he said, 'Don't ask me—don't do it.' I got angry because I wanted an explanation and I wanted to know."

The Argentines plus Skerianz and his attorney drove up from Milan to Geneva on Sunday, February 26, in two cars, one with Giordano, Skerianz, and Marvin Gersten. Maria, Antonio and Petrosino came together in the other car.

On Monday morning, Skerianz and Gersten came to the hotel to have breakfast with the other four before leaving for their 9:00 a.m. meeting with Farina, their Swiss attorney. At Farina's office, Skerianz, Gersten and Farina had a private meeting while Maria and the technicians waited in an outer office. Skerianz emerged from that meeting a short while later to talk to them.

"He [Skerianz] looked relieved. He said everything is going to be okay. Things are better than I thought. Don't worry about anything; everything will go smooth. Go back to the hotel and wait for me there."

Around 10:30 a.m., Skerianz, Farina and Gersten came to the hotel to pick up the others.

Maria recalled, "We all walked towards the Citibank [office building] where the meeting would take place, and we were standing on the corner because it was early—it was raining—and suddenly a man with gray hair and an overcoat came running towards us and said something in Farina's ear. Skerianz said to us, to Giordano, Petrosino, Inigo and I, 'Go to that café over there and wait for me.'"

The man in the overcoat was Farina's private investigator. Walking ahead of the others, he had spotted members of the Swiss police standing in doorways surrounding the Citibank offices. Realizing that his clients were walking into a stakeout, he ran back to warn Farina.

Suddenly, everyone's well-laid plans began unraveling. When Skerianz rejoined the others in the café, he told them to return to the hotel and fetch the luggage. "This arrangement is not going to take place right now," he told them. "We are going back. This is not safe."

Meanwhile, at the Citibank offices, 11 a.m. came and went without any sign of the quarry. The Swiss police stepped up the surveillance in the area and soon spotted Skerianz with two huge briefcases near the hotel. Skerianz had told Inigo and Giordano to bring the cars around from the garage across the street, so the two cars, a Volkswagon Golf and an Alfa Romeo, were pulled up in front of the hotel. The police, monitoring the activity, determined they were going to make a run for it and moved in.

In front of the hotel, Antonio Inigo was sitting in the driver's seat of the Volkswagon, with Skerianz in the back and Maria preparing to get into the car. Giordano was in the driver's seat of the Alfa Romeo and Petrosino was just coming out of the hotel lobby when the police arrived. The police cars came with sirens screaming into the parking lot, tires squealing as police officers jumped from the vehicles, guns drawn. They quickly surrounded the two cars, and the four occupants offered no resistance.

Petrosino, seeing this wild scene unfold before him, turned on his heels and sprinted back through the hotel lobby. He crashed through the kitchen and out of the back door of the hotel, evading capture. Skerianz, Giordano, Antonio and Maria were handcuffed and led away to Champ-Dillon Prison in Geneva. The two attorneys, Gersten and Farina, were nowhere to be found.

Later the same day, in a press conference in Wilmington, Du Pont senior vice president John Malloy and FBI special agent Joseph Corless announced the arrests. As reported by Wilmington's *News Journal* papers, Malloy characterized the stolen documents only as "confidential, proprietary, technical information." Saying it did not cover patented processes, he confirmed it included the kind of secrets on which companies rely for a competitive edge.

"Had the intellectual property described not been recovered," said Malloy, "the company's business performance would have been threatened…the jobs and livelihoods of many of our people jeopardized. In today's competitive world marketplace, intellectual property is the lifeblood of a high-technology company."

The *News Journal* said the officials "seemed to struggle with the question of how the suspects thought they could get away with blackmail when they were willing to accept a check and to identify themselves by signing a contract."

The U.S. Attorney for Delaware, William Carpenter, said the investigation took pains "to convince ourselves that this was not an honest mistake." FBI agent Corless said the suspects might have believed they were safe because they were not in the United States.

Antonio Inigo, Maria de Bianchini, Raul Giordano and Bruno Skerianz now were all subject to extradition proceedings in Geneva, facing extortion charges in the United States carrying penalties of twenty years in prison. When interviewed in the Champ-Dillon Prison by the FBI, Maria, Antonio and Giordano expressed no knowledge of an extortion plot, or even the existence of the documents.

"When I was arrested," Maria said, "I couldn't understand what was happening, why I was there. My only thought was to keep silent about everything so as not to hurt or damage Antonio. I spent 15 days in a jail in Geneva. I got a note from Antonio—the judge gave it to me—asking me to sign extradition papers and go to the USA as soon as possible."

Several days after the arrest, Antonio managed to get another letter to Maria in jail. In it, he said that his nightmare in Milan a few days before their fateful trip was that they were all arrested when they got to Geneva. In Antonio's nightmare, Maria had been wearing her purple sweater.

# WILMINGTON, DELAWARE

Antonio Inigo, Maria de Bianchini and Raul Giordano signed extradition papers and left for trial in the United States. Bruno Skerianz, on the other hand, would fight extradition for the next six months.

Maria recalled, "We were taken to the USA on the same plane, with handcuffs on all the way. We would look at each other and weep. I prayed that my family would not know what was happening. I did not know at that point the news was all over Argentina. When I found out, I wanted to die, my shame was reaching them."

On March 21, 1989, Giordano, de Bianchini and Inigo appeared in Wilmington, Delaware, before U.S magistrate Sue L. Robinson. The U.S. Attorney's office argued there was a risk the three would flee the country, and the magistrate agreed. Bail was denied and Inigo and Giordano were initially sent to Gander Hill Prison in Wilmington. Maria de Bianchini was sent to the Women's Correctional Institution in Claymont, formerly the Woods Haven Kruse School.

None of them were charged with theft of trade secrets, since that event took place in Argentina. Instead, they were all charged with their role in the extortion attempt that took place in Wilmington.

The defendants now found themselves in an environment dominated by their intended victim. The Du Pont Company was the largest employer in Delaware at the time, employing over twenty-five thousand people. The company was also the largest source of tax payments and the largest private property holder in Wilmington. But it was much more than employment or taxes. According to Ralph Nader's book *The Company State*, "Du Pont dominates Delaware as does no single company in any other State—virtually every major aspect of Delaware life…is pervasively and decisively affected by the Du Pont Company, the du Pont family or their agents." Gerald Colby, in his 1984 book *DuPont Dynasty: Behind the Nylon Curtain*, put it more succinctly. "The du Ponts own the State of Delaware."

Now behind bars, separated from her lover and not knowing anyone in this country, Maria relied on her fluency in English to keep from being completely isolated. She arranged to smuggle out letters to Antonio through her cellmate. Her cellmate would include them in letters to her mother, who would then mail them to Antonio. These letters were very private and explicit, an outlet for the despair she was now feeling. These emotional outpourings would emerge to her detriment at the trial.

Each of the three was appointed a local criminal defense attorney by the court. Maria's attorney, Jerome Capone, was a defense lawyer regularly assigned by the federal court to drug and assault cases. He now found himself in the midst of an international extortion case involving one of the world's largest corporations and the largest employer in his home state. Further, his first interviews with his client left him with the feeling that he was only getting part of the story. Considering Maria's access to the documents, her responsibility for them at the plant and their presence with her in Geneva, Capone said later, "To say she had no idea about [the document thefts] just didn't ring true."

Jerome M. Capone, attorney. *Courtesy of Mr. Capone.*

Antonio Inigo faced even greater difficulty because he spoke only Spanish and his court-appointed attorney, Ray Radulski, only English. Antonio was unnerved even further when he found out Radulski was a former corporate lawyer for Du Pont.

"He had just started screaming and weeping. He was flipping out," said Radulski after the trial. "I asked the interpreter why he was acting like this, and she said it was because I had worked for Du Pont. He was sure this was a set-up. Later, the interpreter and I reflected on this scene and she commented, 'We better not tell him my husband works for Du Pont.'"

Maria recalled, "We [Maria and Antonio] met two or three times while at the Marshal's office waiting to be taken into court for various hearings, and we wrote each other letters. Antonio always told me the same thing: don't accept any arrangement or deal; Du Pont won't let us have a fair trial here. I still wanted and loved him, and I didn't want to talk."

On April 6, 1989, the three defendants entered not guilty pleas in the U.S. District Court and were again denied a chance for bail. By the end of April, Jose Petrosino was captured in Italy while trying to rent a car from a rental agency his group had used previously. His lengthy battle against extradition would mean he would miss the trial altogether. While Maria would spend her entire incarceration at the former Woods Haven Kruse School that was being used as a woman's prison, her fellow defendants would be sent to federal corrections prisons in nearby states. Antonio was sent to the FCI in Otisville, New York, a few hours outside of New York City. They would be transported to Delaware for court proceedings.

"Meanwhile," Maria said, "my parents, in Mexico visiting an uncle, sent me a telegram and phoned the jail asking for me. I finally decided to talk to my mother, but I was so ashamed that I wept all the time. The next time my husband answered the phone and he tried to calm me. He wanted to help and wanted me back. He had told the kids all the truth but never put them against me. I talked to my daughter but my son would still not speak to me."

Suddenly, Maria's former life had reopened itself to her. There was a chance she could recapture the things she had given up for Antonio.

## MYSTERY ATTORNEY

A few weeks after he took Maria's case, Capone received a call from an attorney in New Jersey. This attorney reported that he had a friend in Argentina who'd been retained by the families of Maria de Bianchini, Antonio Inigo and Raul Giordano to help with their defense. This Argentine attorney was in the United States and said he wanted to meet with his clients the next day, if Capone could arrange it. Capone agreed and set up the meeting.

The next day Capone met Gerolimo Seminara, a dignified-looking older attorney originally from Sicily. Seminara discovered Capone's family had also come from Sicily, and he remarked good-naturedly how much the two had in common. "Seminara had an old-world gentlemanly quality about him," Capone said later. "I liked him; I thought he could help us gather information in Argentina."

Seminara produced a document written in Spanish that, he assured Capone, said that he had been retained by the three families of the defendants. In fact, Capone later learned that Seminara had approached Maria's husband and offered his services at no cost to him.

In a meeting with the other prisoners Capone and John Malik, Giordano's attorney, were again at a disadvantage because Giordano and Inigo spoke only Spanish. In spite of the language barrier, Capone says he was able to discern that Seminara knew much more about this case than he previously admitted. For one thing, the name of Jose Petrosino, still at large at the time, kept coming up in their conversation. At one point, Capone looked at Seminara and said, "I'm betting that someone in this room has had a cup of coffee with Petrosino." Seminara sidestepped the question, saying, "I talk to his family, and they tell me..."

Woods Haven Kruse School, used as women's prison at the time of this story. *Courtesy of Delaware Public Archives.*

The interview with Maria at the women's prison was conducted in English without any further disagreements among the attorneys. At one point early in the interview, though, Seminara leaned over to Maria and whispered something to her in Spanish. Afterward, Seminara, Capone and Malik met to break down their roles and research assignments in building the defense and parted company.

For several weeks, Capone heard nothing from Seminara about progress on his defense assignments and called Malik to see if he had heard from him. Malik said he had heard from Seminara and told Capone that Seminara didn't trust Capone. Seminara felt that Capone did not treat him with proper respect and didn't want Capone to know everything about the case.

Then Capone went back to Maria to ask her what was going on. Unfortunately, Maria was even more in the dark about Seminara. Although Seminara claimed he was hired by her family, she knew they were too poor to take on such a financial responsibility. And Capone wondered how an experienced international attorney could be jetting back and forth from the United States to South America and Europe on a retainer from a family unable to afford a telephone in their house.

Maria said, "In jail I had time to think everything over, and finally decided I had to go back to my family and try to heal these injuries. They didn't deserve all that shame and pain. I wanted very badly to talk with Antonio about these feelings, but couldn't. I felt being in prison was too high a price for loving a man. I didn't belong there."

Since the first interview with the police in Geneva, Maria continued to maintain that she knew nothing about the documents and nothing about the extortion attempt. Time and again since they had begun discussing the case, Capone had questioned her about the holes and contradictions in her story. He was having a great deal of difficulty building a credible defense, and the pressure was growing inside Maria to tell someone the truth.

"At that point," she said, "I received a terrible letter from my 14-year-old son. He told me I should tell the truth, that he wanted me back with them and their father. He also said that he didn't love me as before because I had lied to them. I knew then I had to tell my attorney the truth sometime soon, stop protecting Antonio and start thinking for myself."

By April 19, Maria was at a breaking point. Capone had been wearing down her resistance to telling him the truth, and on this day he laid it on the line for her.

"Listen," Capone told her, "nobody's going to believe this story about the documents. You're going to be convicted. There are two issues here—one is how did [Skerianz] get the documents; and the second is, were you involved in the extortion conspiracy. You probably weren't involved in the extortion conspiracy, at least until the end.

"But the jury's going to have to decide two things," he said. "The first is how did they come up with the documents, and they're going to think you lied on that one. And if they think you are a liar on that one, they're going to think you're a liar on the ultimate issue [of extortion]. Unless you come clean about these documents, you haven't got a shot.

"You're the least guilty one here," Capone continued. "Look at these phone conversations. [The FBI-taped conversations between Du Pont officials and Skerianz's attorneys to draft the extortion agreement.] Your name doesn't come up until the last day. I think I can get you off, if you can help the government."

Maria, her resistance drained, reluctantly agreed to tell the truth about her involvement and that of the others. She also admitted that Seminara had counseled her not to tell everything she knew to Capone, when he had whispered to her in Spanish at their first meeting. In addition, a family member had told her that Seminara was coming back to Wilmington the next day.

On April 20, Capone was standing in his office on East Eighth Street and Market Street Mall, speaking on the phone and looking distractedly out his second-floor window. There in a window seat at Govatos Restaurant across the street were Seminara and Giordano's wife, Sylvia, eating breakfast. Seminara had brought Sylvia, Maria's friend and companion from Italy, to help him convince Maria that he was representing her best interests. Capone dashed out of his office, down the stairs and across the street and then sauntered by the restaurant to "accidently" spot Seminara. Capone entered the restaurant and was greeted warmly by Seminara, who said he had learned much about the case and that "our people" were not guilty.

Having spent a good part of the previous afternoon finally learning the full story from Maria, Capone was ready to test his fellow attorney. One by one, Capone fed Seminara loaded questions about the case, and at each opportunity, Seminara attempted to mislead him. Convinced now that Seminara's interests differed from those of his client, Capone suggested a meeting of all the defendants. Seminara agreed to this, and Capone returned to his office to set up the meeting.

Capone's first call was to the Assistant U.S. Attorney Edmond Falgowski, who said he would be glad to take up the matter with Seminara in about five minutes, when Seminara was due to meet with him to give a statement

Edmond Falgowski, U.S. attorney. *Courtesy of Mr. Falgowski.*

about the case. Startled, Capone told Falgowski "no way" and raced around the corner from his office to the federal courthouse to cut off Seminara. He made it to the elevator just as Seminara was getting off and then exploded. Capone and Seminara began yelling insults at each other, in two languages, in the hallway of federal courthouse as Seminara tried to get by him to his meeting. "I have this meeting, you're not involved," said Seminara. Capone responded, "You're not going to speak on behalf of my client. If you're going in, I'm going in."

The last part of this scene was played in front of Assistant U.S. Attorney Falgowski, standing at the door of his office. He invited them both in. Fuming, Seminara entered the office and sat opposite Capone. Capone then stood between Seminara and Falgowski and said, "He doesn't represent my client; he doesn't represent anybody. He can't say anything that binds my client."

Seminara stormed from the office, but he was not through. If Maria did not testify against the others, there would be a significantly weaker case against Skerianz and almost no case against the technicians. Seminara wanted to meet with Maria again, and at this point, she wanted to meet with him. Maria was still extremely confused about what was going on and why this attorney supposedly hired by her family was trying to steer her away from the one course of action she thought could save her from a prison term. Seminara had told her not to answer Capone's questions, but Capone was the one person who held out some realistic hope for her to return to her family.

On Friday, April 21, Seminara brought Sylvia Giordano and Raul Giordano's attorney, John Malik, with him for Seminara's final meeting with Maria. Even though Seminara and Maria spoke fluent English, Seminara insisted the meeting be conducted in Spanish. Anticipating this, Capone brought along an interpreter.

Seminara, in an attempt to maintain a solid front among the defendants, pulled out all the emotional stops. "You shouldn't trust this Capone," said Seminara, "I know for a fact he's working for the government. I can't tell you how I know this."

Seminara continued, "Your husband and children have begged me to come up here and talk some sense to you. You're like a drowning sailor and he [Capone] is like the first piece of driftwood you cling to."

While Seminara alternately pleaded with de Bianchini and tore at Capone's credibility, Sylvia Giordano was crying, "Maria, please…"

"Get rid of this Capone; I'll get you a lion of the bar association to come and represent you," said Seminara, as Giordano stared hatefully at Capone.

Through all of this two-hour meeting, Maria repeatedly asked Seminara why she shouldn't trust her attorney. Without saying it directly, Maria intimated that Capone was advising her to turn state's evidence against her fellow defendants. Now afraid that his client's resolve was being worn away by Seminara's incessant hammering, Capone tried a different tack to get her back.

Turning to Sylvia Giordano, Capone asked, "Do you trust the judgment of your husband's attorney?"

"Yes," she said, "he's a good lawyer and is giving good advice."

"Well," said Capone, "ask your attorney if I am trustworthy and a good attorney." Malik confirmed that indeed Capone was trustworthy and a good lawyer.

Maria, her resolve returning, said, "Well, I trust Capone and I'm going to do what he says." At this, Sylvia Giordano began to scream hysterically. Maria de Bianchini had made her final decision, though, and the meeting ended.

Seminara left Wilmington and apparently never returned. "In my opinion," Capone said later, "Seminara had been hired by Skerianz or his partners to keep the others from testifying against him." When he failed, he abandoned the other clients.

Maria had requested that she be allowed to meet with Raul Giordano and Antonio Inigo. She wanted to tell them that she was going to tell the whole story and that they should be able to all go in together. U.S. District Court judge Joseph J. Longobardi refused to allow the meeting. Capone did tell the other defendants' attorneys of her intentions to testify, but Giordano and Inigo refused to change their story.

Unable to bring her co-defendants in with her, Maria met with Assistant U.S. Attorneys Falgowski and Kent Jordan and FBI agent Kirchenbauer for four hours. The FBI and the U.S. Attorney's office offered no deals for her statement—only that whatever she said would not be used against her.

Maria's testimony gave the investigators the day-to-day movements of Skerianz and the three technicians needed to fill in the blanks in their case. Clearly now, the technicians could be tied to the theft of the documents and to their handling during the extortion attempt. Also, Skerianz was identified as the mastermind of the operation.

For several weeks after her testimony, Maria and Capone heard nothing from the prosecutors. Capone continued to visit her at the prison, but the lack of activity on the government's part was shaking Maria's confidence in her decision. Expecting at least for his client to be let out on bail, Capone filed a motion in court for her release. Finally, the U.S. Attorney's office contacted him and said, "We're dropping all charges against her."

After four and a half months in the women's prison, Maria was released but not freed entirely. Because she was named a material witness in the case, she was restricted to the Wilmington area. As a foreigner with no local friends or family, she could be retained in prison if she had nowhere to stay. Capone arranged for an Argentine woman working for Catholic Social Services to take her in as a boarder. For several months until the trial, Maria lived quietly in the woman's home in Elsmere. She was not allowed to have money or be out of the house after 6:00 p.m.

In September 1989, Skerianz lost his extradition battle and was sent to Wilmington to stand trial. At his bail hearing, he pleaded innocent and said he had been only following the advice of his attorneys. Bail was denied and in mid-October his privately retained attorney, Richard Zappa, filed for a change in venue. Citing tremendous pretrial publicity and the pervasive influence of the Du Pont Company in Wilmington, Zappa claimed Skerianz could not get a fair trial here. The motion was denied, and Skerianz joined his former recruits on trial for extortion.

## THE TRIAL

Honorable Kent A. Jordan, former U.S. attorney, now Federal Appellate Court judge, Third Circuit. *Courtesy of Judge Jordan.*

The trial got underway in U.S. District Court in Wilmington in December 1989 and lasted through two weeks of testimony and argument. The evidence against Skerianz was relatively straightforward, but it was much less so for Inigo and Giordano. In their defense attorneys' eyes, there was no physical evidence of their involvement in the extortion attempt other than their having been in Geneva with Skerianz. It was up to the prosecution to prove they were involved. Testimony from a Swiss financial police unit member that described the arrest setup and execution undermined the defense position of ordinary business negotiations going on, according to U.S. Attorney Kent Jordan.

Maria said, "Till the very end I wished I wouldn't have to do it. I wished and prayed that Antonio would tell the truth himself and spare me. I wished I could have the opportunity to talk to him, but I wasn't allowed."

It was Maria's testimony that was most damaging to her former lover and his fellow technician. Previous government testimony had focused on handwriting and fingerprint analysis to show the technicians' handling of the document, which could have occurred at virtually any time. She showed the technicians were actively involved with Skerianz just prior to their arrest in Geneva by detailing the facts about the document thefts and their work in Italy reviewing and collating them.

"I felt I was betraying him when I testified," Maria said. "There was hate in him, I could feel it. During my testimony my legs were trembling. I couldn't stop looking at Antonio; his eyes were full of anger and hate."

"The jury was riveted on Maria because Maria and Antonio were looking at each other. Their expressions spoke volumes," said U.S. attorney Edmond Falgowski. "She was anguished, he was angry."

Antonio told his attorney, Ray Radulski, about the love letters from Maria during a break in the trial and about one letter in particular he received shortly before she turned state's evidence. Radulski, anxious to introduce something damaging to the government's star witness, went to the federal marshal's office to root through Antonio's belongings. There, among the sneakers and sweatshirts, he found the letter he wanted. Rushing back to his office, he got an interpreter to translate the letter and then brought it to court.

Radulski focused his cross-examination of Maria on attacking her credibility. The government had admitted in the opening statements that initially she had lied to investigators about the case, but the jury was expected to believe she was now telling the truth. "You lied to Charre?" Radulski asked, referring to her former boss at Ducilo. "You lied to your family? You lied to the Swiss police?" Maria admitted as much to each question.

Then Radulski introduced the March 28 letter she had written from prison. "Would you please attempt an English translation of only the highlighted portion of that letter," he said.

Maria read, "I'm innocent and I'm not going to negotiate anything, even though I would sell my soul for leaving this place." Then she commented, "Something like that."

"When you say you would sell your soul to leave this place, what do you mean by that?" Radulski asked.

"I didn't mean I would sell my soul—that is something I wrote—I mean that it was a terrible place to be in, I was suffering. I didn't want to be there—I didn't feel that I had to be there. I didn't feel I belonged in prison," she replied.

"Did you mean that you would cheat, that you would steal, and that you would lie, that you would do anything to get out of jail?" continued Radulski.

"No, sir. I was there because I was protecting him," Maria answered.

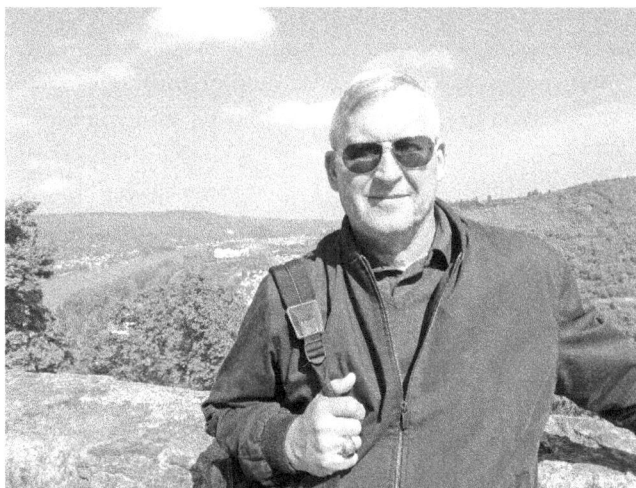

Raymond M. Radulski, attorney. *Courtesy of Mr. Radulski.*

Maria's credibility with the jury withstood the cross-examination, and generally, she had come across as a nice person caught up in a tangled web of events. Her testimony was damaging to Skerianz but devastating to Antonio. The trial ended in December 1989 with guilty verdicts handed down against all three defendants. Antonio was led away from the court, cursing Maria.

Maria was free at last to leave the United States. Her husband had forgiven her and was welcoming her back, though she still had misgivings. Her uncle in Mexico City had offered to put her up there and bring her children to live with her. But that was something to consider in the future. Now Christmas Eve was approaching, and she wanted to return home. Her uncle had promised to send her airfare home, but it could not arrive in time for her flight.

Fortuitously, a Du Pont attorney telephoned Capone and asked if there was anything they could do for Maria in gratitude for her testimony. As a matter of fact, there was, Capone told him. So, Maria de Bianchini—former lover of Antonio Inigo and indicted extortionist against Du Pont—was flown back to her husband in Argentina using money loaned to her by the Du Pont Company.

## AFTERMATH

Shortly after the guilty verdicts were handed down, Raul Giordano admitted to his pre-sentence officer that he had taken documents from the Ducilo plant. Antonio Inigo still denied taking any documents himself but said he asked Maria to smuggle out some documents, which he said she did.

Giordano and Inigo were sentenced to three and a half years in prison. Bruno Skerianz was sentenced to six and a half years in prison.

The Du Pont Company basked in the glow of a successful sting operation. Jack F. Schmutz, senior vice president of the company's legal department, characterized the affair as "exciting as hell" when interviewed by the *Wilmington News Journal*. "Right out of a Ken Follett novel," he said.

In Singapore, construction continued on Du Pont's newest Lycra plant, its ninth.

Maria de Bianchini returned to her family in Mercedes, Argentina. She said,

> *I received a letter from Antonio in June* [1990], *accusing me of being a liar. It was full of hate, curses and threats. He is strong in his hate and I am still*

*weak. I wish I could hate him or feel anger—that would be healthier. I won't answer it, though that is what he wants and I want, in a way.*

*We had good moments, but on balance, our four months together were kind of a nightmare. I still don't know what happened, why we weren't getting along as we expected or dreamed. I think I was so weak and in pain, I needed him so much to protect me and support me, and he couldn't take it.*

*I don't know what will happen in the future; sometimes I am a little scared because he will come back to Mercedes, sooner or later.*

On February 1, 1991, in an amazing turnabout that had members of the Delaware legal community buzzing, the U.S. Court of Appeals for the Third Circuit reversed the convictions of Raul Giordano and Antonio Inigo, holding that the evidence of their participation in the extortion attempt was insufficient.

The Court of Appeals said, in part, "This record shows only that Inigo and Giordano misappropriated Du Pont's trade secrets and violated their original agreements not to compete in order to gain employment with PNB [a partnership owned by Skerianz and two others]….It does not show they intended to threaten Du Pont with economic harm unless they were paid off, or knowingly participated with Skerianz in a scheme to extort." Edmond Falgowski would summarize the court ruling years later, saying, "It was not enough to be present. There was no evidence they knew of extortion."

The same appeal sent Bruno Skerianz back to U.S. District Court for resentencing under the federal blackmail guidelines.

On March 1, 1991, two years and one day after his arrest in Geneva, Antonio Inigo was released from federal prison in Michigan to return home to his wife and family in Argentina.

"I paid and still am paying a very high price for loving and following him, but it was my choice," Maria Inez Lorenzo de Bianchini said.

In retrospect, both prosecuting attorneys Edmond Falgowski and Kent Jordan, now a federal appellate court judge, agreed this type of crime would not be repeated today. There would be no smuggling of pilfered documents by the suitcase load. Instead, a computer hacker would attempt to accomplish the same crime sitting alone in his basement.

# BIBLIOGRAPHY

## BOOKIES, BAWDY HOUSES AND CHIEF BLACK

### *Books and Publications*

Downey, Dennis B. "'Mercy, Master, Mercy': Racial Politics and the Lynching of George White." *Delaware History* 20, no. 3 (2003).

Frank, Bill. *Bawds and Police: Bill Frank's Delaware*. Wilmington, DE: Middle Atlantic Press, 1987.

Hoffecker, Carol. *Corporate Capital, Wilmington in the Twentieth Century*. Philadelphia: Temple University Press, 1983.

Morris, Edmund. *Theodore Rex*. New York: Random House, 2001.

### *Documents*

Annual Report of the Department of Public Safety, FY 1897. Historical Society of Delaware.

Charles Powell Testimony to Grand Jury, April 1936. Attorney General P. Warren Green Administrative Files. Delaware Public Archives.

C.S. Morford to H.S. Schutt, president of Directors of Public Safety, November 30, 1936. Wilmington City Solicitor Records. Delaware Public Archives.

Deposition of Edna Powell, July 24, 1936. Attorney General P. Warren Green Administrative Files. Delaware Public Archives.

Deposition of Harold Witsil, August 7, 1936. Attorney General P. Warren Green Administrative Files. Delaware Public Archives.

George "Shelley" Fisher Affidavit, August 10, 1936. Wilmington City Solicitor Records. Delaware Public Archives.

Letter from C.S. Morford to Willard F. Deputy, IRS, December 9, 1936. Wilmington City Solicitor Records. Delaware Public Archives.

Letter to P.W. Green from R.E. Vetterli, FBI., August 19, 1936. Attorney General P. Warren Green Administrative Files. Delaware Public Archives.

Letter, J.E. Hoover to Superintendent Black, November 23, 1936. Wilmington City Solicitor Records. Delaware Public Archives.

Letter, Superintendent Black to J.E. Hoover, FBI., November 19, 1936. Wilmington City Solicitor Records. Delaware Public Archives.

Report by Lieutenant James C. Riley to City Solicitor, August 17, 1936. Wilmington City Solicitor Records. Delaware Public Archives.

Report of Detective Wallace and Riley to City Solicitor Morford, August 14, 1936. Wilmington City Solicitor Records. Delaware Public Archives.

Report of Detective Wallace to C.S. Morford, September 11, 1936. Wilmington City Solicitor Records. Delaware Public Archives.

Report of Private Investigator to C.S. Morford, October 2, 1936. Wilmington City Solicitor Records. Delaware Public Archives.

Statement from Officer Palmer Walls, January 27, 1937. Wilmington City Solicitor Records. Delaware Public Archives.

Statement of Edna Powell, December 9, 1936. Wilmington City Solicitor Records. Delaware Public Archives.

Statement of Patrolman James Wilson to C.S. Morford, August 24, 1936. Wilmington City Solicitor Records. Delaware Public Archives.

Statement to the Board of Pardons of the State of Delaware, filed by H. Albert Young on behalf of Edna Powell, April 23, 1938. Wilmington City Solicitor Records. Delaware Public Archives.

William Powell Testimony to Grand Jury, May 13, 1936. Attorney General P. Warren Green Administrative Files. Delaware Public Archives.

## *Newspapers*

*Delmarva Sunday Morning Star*, August 2, 1936; December 6, 1936.

*Journal Every Evening*, June 23, 1903; December 9, 1936; December 10, 1936; December 10, 1940.

*Wilmington Morning News*, January 29 and 30, 1902; April 1, 1936; May 1, 1936; May 20, 1936; July 31, 1936; August 1, 1936; August 4, 1936; August 7, 1936; December 2, 1936; December 5, 1936; December 9, 1936; March 3, 1937; January 8, 1938; August 1942.

## *Interviews by the Author*

Biondi, O. Frank, December 2009.
Herlihy, Honorable Jerome O., December 2008.
Herlihy, Thomas, III, December 2008.
Jamison, Joseph, August 2008.
Jones, Jane Riley, July 2008.
McLaughlin, Mayor William T., December 2007.
Monahan, Thomas, May 2009.
Quill, Leonard, July 2008.
Quinn, Kevin, July 2009.

# THREE GUN WILSON AND THE END OF PROHIBITION IN DELAWARE

## *Books and Publications*

Association Against the Prohibition Amendment. "Food for Thought, What Prohibition Has Done for Us." Delaware Division AAPA, Hagley Museum and Library.

Cardwell, Robert G. *Penology in Delaware: A History of the First State*. Vol. 2. New York: Lewis Historical Publishing Company, 1947.

Dighe, Dr. Ranjit. S. "Pierre S. du Pont and the Making of an Anti-Prohibition Activist." *Social History of Alcohol and Drugs* 24, no. 2 (Summer 2010): 97–118.

Gourvish, Terence. "The Business of Alcohol in the United States and the United Kingdom." *Business and Economic History* 26, no. 2 (Winter 1997).

History of Alcohol Prohibition. National Commission on Marihuana and Drug Abuse. www.druglibrary.org/schaffer/library/studies.

Hu, T. *The Liquor Tax in the U.S.: 1791–1947*. New York: Columbia University Press, 1950.

Medkeff, John Jr., *Brewing in Delaware*. Charleston, SC: Arcadia Publishing, 2015.

Okrent, Daniel. *Last Call: The Rise and Fall of Prohibition*. New York: Scribner, 2010.

Palmer, Scott. "The Klair Law." *Millcreek Hundred History* (blog), January 4, 2012. mchistory.blogsppot.com.

Reed, H. Clay, ed. *Delaware: A History of the First State*. Vol. 1. New York: Lewis Historical Publishing Company, 1947.

Standard Distributing Company. StandardDE.com.

Wilson, Harold D. *Dry Laws and Wet Politicians*. Somerville, MA: Pequa Press, 1922.
———. *Dry Law Facts Not Fiction*. Newark, DE: Press of Kells, 1931.

## Documents

House Substitute for House Bill No. 312, An Act Creating a Commission for the Control of the Manufacture, Sale and Transportation of Liquor, Wines and Beer. Hagley Museum and Library.
U.S. District of Delaware Criminal Case Files 1829–1974 #43, 1930, December Term. *U.S. of A v. Democratic League of Delaware*, a corporation of the State of Delaware. National Archives and Records Administration.

## Newspapers

*Columbia Daily Telegram*, July 1, 1942.
*Delmarva Star/Sunday Morning Star*, November 2, 1930; January 11, 1931; April 12, 1931; October 25, 1931; December 13, 1931; December 20, 1931; December 27, 1931.
*Evening Journal*, February 7, 1931; February 19, 1931; February 20, 1931; January 8, 1932; January 11, 1932.
*Pittsburgh Press*, May 16, 1930; July 16, 1930; September 24, 1930. Carnegie Library of Pittsburgh.
*Santa Cruz Sentinel-News*, September 22, 1945.
*Wilmington Morning News*, September 27, 1930; October 27, 1930; November 20, 1930; November 26, 1930; December 5, 1963; September 27, 1987.

## Interview by the Author

Kelly, Michael P., December 2014.

# THE COP AND THE INCORRIGIBLE

## Documents

Federal Bureau of Investigation Report to Frank J. Mahoney, Chief of Police, January 8, 1947. Conaty family records.
Investigation Report, Wilmington Police Department, Case B-32023. Conaty family records.

Minutes of Police Pension Board, January 15, 1947; February 19, 1947; November 19, 1952. City of Wilmington Treasurer's Office.

Report of Autopsy, Delaware Medical Examiner, P.M. Rovitti, Examining Physician. Conaty family records.

Statement of Daniel Norris, Wilmington Police Department, December 27, 1946. Conaty family records.

Statement of Detective Frank Miller, Wilmington Police Department, December 26, 1946. Conaty family records.

Statement of Leonard Aubrey Bushell, Wilmington Police Department, December 26, 1946. Conaty family records.

## *Newspapers*

*Delmarva Star*, July 12, 1931; July 19, 1931; February 9, 1947.

*Journal Every Evening*, July 11, 1945; August 27, 1945; December 12, 1945; December 22, 1945; January 18, 1946; August 18, 1946; December 30, 1946; December 26, 1946; December 27, 1946; January 4, 1947; February 7, 1947; February 8, 1947; February 14, 1947; February 15, 1947; October 27, 1949; October 28, 1949; October 29, 1949.

*Philadelphia Inquirer*, December 28, 1946.

*Wilmington Morning News/News Journal*, July 14, 1944; December 12, 1945; December 13, 1945; December 14, 1945; January 21, 1946; December 27, 1946; February 6, 1947; April 8, 1947; September 10, 1965; September 13, 1965; June 11, 1966; February 20, 1967; October 5, 1981; August 14, 1982; November 16, 1989.

## *Interviews by the Author*

Conaty, Louise, Wachter Hoffman and William Conaty, March 2000.

Conaty, Thomas, III, and Gerard Conaty, February 2000.

McLaughlin, George, February 2000.

# BAD CHOICES

## *Books and Publications*

Brandt, Charles. *I Heard You Paint Houses*. Hanover, NH: Steerforth Press, 2004.

## Documents

Autopsy 73-705, Fred Gawronski, by Ali Z. Hameli, MD, Examining Physician. Delaware Public Archives.

Criminal Action No. 1888, Transcript of Trial Record and File Volume A, January 14, 1974, through Volume E January 18, 1974, *State of Delaware v. Thomas Bowie Barker Defendant*. DPA.

Statement of Phyllis Holmes, taken by Detective T.A. Koston. DPA.

Superior Court Docket 950, Criminal Action 1974, *State of Delaware vs. Thomas B. Barker, Alice Gawronski*. DPA.

## Newspapers

*Arizona Republic*, November 17, 2006. Yellowfootprints.com.

*Wilmington News Journal*, October 25, 1973; October 27, 1973; January 15, 1974; January 16, 1974; January 17, 1974; January 18, 1974; January 19, 1974; May 17, 1991; May 18, 1991; May 21, 1991; May 22, 1991; May 23, 1991; May 24, 1991; May 29, 1991; May 30, 1991; May 31, 1991; June 2, 1991.

## Interviews by the Author

Branch, Alice Gawronski, December 2012, August 2013, November 2013.

Brandt, Charles, July 2013.

Hurley, Joseph A., June 2013.

Tucker, Michael, July 2013.

Weiner, Jeffrey, July 2013.

# LOVE, LIES AND LYCRA SECRETS

## Books and Publications

Colby, Gerard. *Du Pont Dynasty: Behind the Nylon Curtain*. Secaucus, NJ: Lyle Stuart, 1984. [Quote taken from defense attorney motion for Change of Venue.]

Moser, Penny Ward. "A Long Stretch of the Imagination." *Sports Illustrated*, February 12, 1990.

Phelan, James, and Robert C. Pozen, *The Company State: Ralph Nader's Study Group Report on DuPont in Delaware.* Introduction by Ralph Nader. New York: Grossman, 1973. [Quote taken from defense attorney motion for Change of Venue.]

## Documents

Affidavit by Charles Flagg, Special Agent. Federal Bureau of Investigation.
Letter from Maria de Bianchini to Jerome Capone, June 18, 1990.
Letter (translation) from Maria de Bianchini to Antonio Inigo.
Motion for Change of Venue, submitted by attorneys Richard A. Zappa and Melanie K. Sharp for Bruno Skerianz to Judge Joseph J. Longobardi, October 18, 1989.
Opinion of the Court, United States Court of Appeals for the Third Circuit. *Appellee, v. Antonio Inigo, Raul Armando Giordano, Bruno Skerianz, Appellants,* February 1, 1991.
Trial Transcript, *United States of America v. Bruno Skerianz, Raul Armando Giordano and Antonio Ruben Inigo,* Volume G and H, December 12 and 13, 1989.

## Newspapers

*New York Times*, March 28, 1988.
*Wilmington News Journal*, December 20, 1989; March 19, 1990; February 2, 1991; May 2, 1991.

## Interviews by the Author

Capone, Jerome, January 1990, March 1990, March 1991.
Falgowski, Edmond, August 2020.
Jordan, Honorable Kent A., September 2020.
Radulski, Raymond M., February 1990, February 1991, September 2020.

# ABOUT THE AUTHOR

A lifelong Wilmingtonian Kevin McGonegal attended St. Edmond's and Archmere Academies before earning his bachelor's degree in history from Fairfield University. He worked in Wilmington's Mayor's Office under Mayors Tom Maloney, Bill McLaughlin and Dan Frawley, including stints as director of OMB and mayor's chief of staff. He spent thirty-three years as a broker in Wilmington's commercial real estate market, along with co-teaching a course for twenty years in the University of Delaware's Master's in Public Administration Program. Currently, he serves on the boards of the Delaware Historical Society and Wilmington's Downtown Visions. He and his wife, Cindy, split their time between Wilmington and Lewes, Delaware.

www.ingramcontent.com/pod-product-compliance
Lightning Source LLC
Chambersburg PA
CBHW060343100426
42812CB00003B/1112